The Color of My Paint

MARIO L. VAZQUEZ

THE COLOR OF MY PAINT

2009

The Color of My Paint

CONTENTS

ACKNOWLEDGMENTS

I would not have completed this project without the support and encouragement of the great people in my life, particularly my family, friends, teachers, colleagues, and students: You have all made me who I am today. I want to especially recognize my son, Mario Jr., for giving me the joy and spirit of being a child all over again through him. You will have many memorable stories of your own to share when you become an adult. I want to thank my mother, Maria Lopez, for everything she has done for me over the years; love you, Ma. To Idalia Rivera, for helping me stay focused during my childhood school years and for going the extra mile for my education. To Arlene Hadipour, for always believing in me and being there for me spiritually. Special thanks to Leonard Nash, who provided editorial assistance, professional guidance and positive support to my material. Thanks to my great friends, Cathy Ahmed, Julio Cruz, Federico Csapek, Melinda Hernandez, Oswald Hernandez, Billy Jones, Mayra Muñoz, and Yuri Romaniuk. To the "Dream Team" members, Marjorie Gomez, Toby Hernandez, and Vicky Rodriguez. Thanks to Ray Azcuy, William Chiodo, and Mabel Morales, for being great supporters of the art world in the Miami-Dade County Public Schools. Thanks to the Dade Art Educators Association for continuously supporting and advocating for the Arts in the Miami-Dade County District. To all of the students, teachers, and administrators that have been part of the great family of

Hialeah-Miami Lakes Senior High School. To my professors in the Art Education department at Southern Connecticut State University for providing me with the knowledge and inspiration to become an Art educator, Dr. Kathy Connors, Dr. Don Cyr, Dr. Arthur Guagliumi, and Dr. Chuck Wieder. Thanks to Dr. Kyra Belan, Alfred Keller, and Gladys Velazquez for being great supporters of the Arts and superb professors at Broward College. Thank you all for providing me with great support and for keeping me focused on *my* dream. I want to thank the many writers who have inspired me over the years, and especially two gentlemen who have had a great impact on me through their own books: Mario Luis Kreutzberger Blumenfeld, television host, who has brought joy and laughter into my family's living room every Saturday evening for the past twenty-plus years via his show *Sábado Gigante*; and Joel Osteen, pastor, who brings joy and the spirit of the Lord into my heart every Sunday from Lakewood Church. Thanks to all of my students, especially those who have elected art to be a permanent part of their lives—Pedro Alvarez, Allan Bueno, Gustavo Cervantes, Jonathan Gomez, Yoelmir Santana, Amliv Sotomayor, and Cristina Urdaneta—your success stories are the true reason and passion for my calling to teach. To Pedro Alvarez, thank you for taking on the challenge of designing the cover of this book; your art will live forever. Thank you all for being such an inspiration and for giving me the encouragement to complete this project.

I Dedicate This Book To

Abuela Luisa

I Know You Are Watching Over Me From Heaven.
Your Love Will Always Live In My Heart.

And To My Son,

Mario Jr.

Who Forever Reminds Me That There Is A Child
In Every One Of Us That Never Grows Up.

PREFACE

I was inspired to write these stories as a means of sharing with readers the life-changing experiences that have molded me into who I am today. *The Color of My Paint* is a compilation of my childhood experiences and adventures that would become my life lessons. I learned the lessons suggested by each story through real-life experiences. The stories are not intended to inspire readers to engage in such childish behavior, but readers can learn from my experiences just the same. My family, friends, colleagues, and students are all part of my inspiration to share these stories. I have always been an adventurer at heart and have enjoyed learning something every day. As a little boy, I imagined traveling around the world. Traveling, through either physical or mental activity, has always been a treasured experience for me. I hope my stories rekindle memories of your own childhood, and will inspire you to learn continually throughout your life. Moments of wisdom and enlightenment can happen in a flash. When looking back, you will see that mistakes are lessons in disguise, and that the people who come into your life are there to teach you something lacking in your existence. Cherish every moment as a learning experience, an opportunity to grow mentally and spiritually. When recalling your memories, you will understand that every moment happens for a reason.

"My love for animals has developed strongly,
and I have grown to understand their existence as our
counterparts in sharing our small little world."

THE CREATURE WITHOUT A TAIL

On one of those hot and humid Saturday mornings in Hato Rey, Puerto Rico, I woke up and cleaned my room, which I shared with my older brother, Luis, and then I went outside to play in our backyard. In those years, there was a neighbor boy, about my age, who often played with his imaginary friend on the other side of the fence. Sometimes he would play with a stick, pretending it was a sword and pretending to be dressed as a knight in armor. Actually, he would wear a paper hat and a dress-up uniform he constructed of paper scraps and broken toys.

I sometimes interrupted his sword fighting with his imaginary friend for good purposes. I would customarily approach the fence and ask him if I could have some *acerolas*.[1] I loved the taste of this small fruit, red as a cherry and big as a nickel. Not having an *acerola* tree on our side of the fence upset me. After a brief encounter with the make-believe medieval knight, I wandered to the back of the house to explore the natural environment more closely.

When the wind blew, the entire backyard made strange noises. The back of our house had a large attached shack we called the *marquesina*.[2] We used this large open space for family gatherings and as a covered parking area for our cars. The noise came from the trees, the dried banana plant leaves, and the creaking of the old wood and metal roof. It was at times a scary mix of strange noises. Running through the backyard, I would inspect how tall the plants had grown since my last visit. I would go to the lemon tree, smell the lemons, and inspect them to see if they were ready to be picked. I would also smell the *recao*,[3] which my family added to the *sofrito*[4] when cooking various dishes. The smell in the yard was distinctive. The yard was my interesting little tropical world.

During my exploration of our jungle-looking yard, I would also observe the creek behind the fence that divided the back property. Some days it would be dried up, but other times the water would flow as if a torrential storm had just passed. Many creatures lived in the yard, which also kept me on high alert. I would see many large toads, *coquis*[5], spiders, red giant ants, bees, worms, and flies.

There were many birds that visited the grounds and also ate the fruit from the trees. Among these were the *Reinitas*,[6] small, cheerful black and yellow birds. The pigeons made a low noise resembling that of an owl, and the hummingbirds flew around, peeking inside the flowers. After periods of drought, the clay soil took on a leathery look and feel, becoming as dry and brittle as desert ground.

Our yard also contained iguanas of various sizes and many shades of green. Some looked scary and others looked friendly. The tongues of the large iguanas went in and out as the mysterious creatures searched for food. Some were as small as three inches long, but some were as big as three feet long. When I first saw the biggest one, my heart pounded faster and faster. I started sweating as I stared at it. When I saw a large iguana at other times, sometimes I would wait for it to come towards me, but I usually ended up chasing it.

When the iguanas ran through the yard, they moved the dried banana leaves and made a wispy, crackling sound resembling that of a rattlesnake. I would be so afraid, and my fear once again would haunt me as I heard them moving in the yard. During one particular chase of a large iguana, I had a plowing tool in my hand, it was a long stick with a bended sharp metal piece at the end used to move dirt and loosen it for planting. I stopped when the iguana stopped, and I was so scared that I closed my eyes and swung the tool at it. I paused and heard nothing for a second. I suddenly felt drops of water splash on my face and hands. When I opened my eyes, I went into a sort of trance. I couldn't believe my eyes for a moment. They were wide open, and my jaw dropped as low as it could. The wet droplets that I felt on my face and hands were not water or rain. They were actually dark red blood from the iguana. I really just wanted to scare it and my intention was never to hurt or kill the iguana.

When I saw the blood and the iguana's tail, detached from its little body and jumping around, I panicked and went into a mild state of shock. The iguana ran one way and I ran to the other side of the yard. Seeing the blood made me scared and weak. The iguana left a trail of blood. After running around the yard for several minutes, I ended up on the other side of the house. When my heart calmed down, I grabbed a tree branch from the ground, closed my eyes, and started praying. I prayed that I hadn't killed the poor defenseless iguana. It was about five minutes later that I opened my eyes. The first things I saw when I opened them were the many trees and a metal cylinder as tall as I was.

When I tapped on the cylinder, it made a sound as loud as Sunday morning church bells. The noise I was making had a soothing effect that mentally took me to a distant land. I couldn't believe I was making such a noise with a dried-up tree branch. I closed my eyes and kept hitting the metal cylinder, imagining it was a large bell calling people to Sunday mass.

Pausing, then hitting it again, pausing and hitting…just like the loud town church bells I heard every week in the distance.

When I opened my eyes, I was surprised by a pair of angry eyes staring at me. The older, short, chubby lady, who wore a long dress with an apron over it, surprised me by loudly shouting what in my crazy little mind was I doing. She was my grandmother's older sister, Mama Gume. I was not aware that the metal cylinder I had been tapping with all my heart was the metal tank that provided gas to the kitchen stove. While she screamed with anger, she also had a shocked look, as if the tank might explode and kill both of us. She looked at the bloody trail on the cement that came from the back of the house. She asked me why there was such a trail of blood on the ground. I confessed that I had attacked an iguana by mistake, and said that I had been scared that it was going to attack me. She told me that in all her long life she had never heard of an iguana attacking a human. Then she explained to me that the attack was evil and that I should not repeat it. As a punishment, I was immediately sent to my room for the rest of the day.

Later that day, Mama Gume was not angry with me anymore. She explained that many animals were defenseless, and that attacking them was like hurting someone you loved. She asked how I would like someone hurting me and running away. It was not right to hurt animals, especially the ones that lived in her backyard. I learned a valuable lesson that day: not to hurt animals, and to love them as they were my friends.

I soon developed a love for animals and small creatures, but I must confess that to this day, reptiles are not my favorite. In my opinion, they are scary and not too attractive, but of course that is no excuse for harming them.

As part of my weekend routine, after cleaning and organizing my room, the yard visit continued to be a ritual. Two weeks later, as I inspected the trees that gave us lemons from which we made homemade juice, I saw the iguana whose tail I had accidentally cut off. The tail had grown back to about one-third of its original length. I stared at it and said in my mind that I was sorry about what had happened. It looked at me and continued moving into the tall grass. I ran to Mama Gume and told her what I had just seen. She told me that iguanas grow their tails back, but that didn't change the fact that I had hurt it. She also told me that just like humans, animals feel pain and suffer greatly when injured, and are even scared for the rest of their lives after an experience like that. She told me to be good to animals because even though we might think they are not watching, animals have a way of sensing a dangerous and evil person. She said to love them and they would love me back.

From that day on, my love for animals has developed strongly, and I have grown to understand their existence as our counterparts in sharing our small little world. Of course I never repeated the iguana experience. In fact, until now I have kept it to myself due to my guilty conscience. I don't believe Mama Gume ever told anyone either about the embarrassing way that I had reacted to my own insecurities in the backyard. However, I discovered that iguanas are harmless to humans and that their tails can grow back. I had feared that something might happen to me for hurting the iguana, but then everything changed and all my worries vanished. As time passed, the yard trees and plants grew taller and stronger. The yard, which had been my secret labyrinth, became a safe haven and a peaceful place for me to explore. The experience with the iguana also helped me learn that humans and nature are the perfect combination when coexisting in harmony.

"I was not looking to become a businessman –
I was interested in becoming an artist."

THE COLOR OF MY PAINT

For many people, shells on the beach are artifacts of a past existence. At one point in time, a creature lived within the confines of each hard shell, deep within the waters of the sea. When the ocean water pushes them to the shore, they become trapped by the dry sand and unable to swim back to the water. When they are dried up due to the heat of the hot sun bearing down on their thin yet beautiful shapes, they are transformed into the skeletons that are the beauty of our curiosity.

I have always been inquisitive and curious when it comes to things of nature and animals. Why did shells become objects of my curiosity? Why do they have so many shapes and forms? On one summer day during our family visits to Seaside Park Beach in Bridgeport, Connecticut, I went towards the water along the shore by myself and began to pick up many different types of shells. They were dried up and consisted of the most beautiful variety of colors I saw on the small sea clams, starfish, corals, ark shells, scallops, tiger moon, and nautical shells.

When I gathered enough to fill my hands, I would go back to my parents and ask for a bag to put them in. I had collected enough shells to make the bag heavy and prone to break. When it was time to leave, I was very protective of the shells to make sure they did not break. I had them at arms reach to make sure they survived the trip back home without breaking or chipping.

When I got home, I took them to the bathroom and put them in the bathtub to rinse off the sand. One by one, the water washed away the accumulated sand and algae. I had a picture in my mind with all the shells having different colors and patterns similar to those seen through a kaleidoscope. One was a shiny light brown color, and was the one that stood out the most. I put it to the side while I made sure the rest were thoroughly cleaned. An idea came to me that became the starting point of my admiration, inspiration, and calling to create art.

After the shells dried, I went to my room and pulled out a pack of school paints and markers. I took the biggest shell, which resembled a clam. It had a large white area I could draw and paint on. Suddenly, my creativity was born—onto this hard white shell. I wanted to give it life again with paint. The colors of my paints were blue, brown, and yellow. With these colors I created a landscape on the shell. I created more and more designs, painting on all of the shells. Suddenly, the shells became my canvas, and my imagination was my limit.

It took me several days to complete all the shells. When I laid them out on the kitchen floor, I saw a multitude of interesting abstract designs. I got an idea that later became appealing to many people. I used to see other kids my age around town selling lemonade to the people passing by on the sidewalk. The kids would have a table with lemonade, ice, sugar, and plastic cups. My idea was a little out of the ordinary. I used four of the milk crates that my brother and I kept our toys in. I took the milk crates to the sidewalk and placed our green chalkboard across them, creating a small table.

I put all the shells with the best designs on my improvised table, and placed a piece of paper with "ten cents" written on it on the front side. It was early afternoon and a few people passed by. Some took a look, but they all kept on walking. An hour or so later, more people walked by, as it was around the time most people got home from their jobs. My first customer looked at one, picked it up, and asked me what he could use the painted shell for. I told the tall man that the large shell could be used as an ashtray, and when not being used it could be turned over and transformed into a work of art. Those words must have convinced him, because he agreed to buy that shell, and others as well. To this day, I don't know why I said that or what inspired me to say such a thing. I just knew that my goal was to sell my art. The large shells were ten cents and the small ones were five cents. I sold about two handfuls. That was the first and last time I ever sold shells on the sidewalk. I felt I needed more polished persuasive skills to sell my art so I decided to never doing it again.

I gave the light brown shell that stood out from the others to my second grade teacher. It was a week later that my older brother, Steven, gave me a piece of mail. We both were curious about who it was from. It was a small envelope with nice handwriting, addressed to me. He thought it was from a girlfriend or a secret admirer. He bothered me until I finally opened it. It was a letter from my teacher, thanking me for giving her the shell. She had added the shell to her shell collection. I was surprised because I didn't know she had a shell collection, and I was happy that she had taken the time to send me a letter. It was my first piece of mail. From that day on, the shells inspired me to create other pieces of artwork. Because the shells project required me to visit the beach more often, and my parents had busy schedules and could not always take me there, I had to look for other means to create art.

While growing up my father was a strict parent and an old fashion mannered man. He tended to correct us for anything we did wrong and even the rights things. When we ate supper we had to make sure our left hand was not on the table. When he talked to us we needed to look him straight in the eyes. He would always tell us that children were little people and should act as disciplined as adults. All his attention leaned toward my brother, Luis, and at times this was to my advantage because I could do things in the yard without being constantly questioned. I later understood his demeanor and also learned that his father was very strict with him, so being strict with us was something normal for him. In spite of his parenting skills, he believed we should be rewarded for good behavior and for helping with chores around the house. As a weekend ritual he would take us to the toy store or the supermarket and buy one item for each of us. At the toy store, my brother and I would pick plastic model cars. They came in many pieces, so handling the tiny parts required great patience and care. The small plastic pieces were thin and fragile. It would take us several days to complete the project of putting all the pieces together. Gradually, my brother and I created an impressive collection of model cars, but we could not play with the cars because they could break easily. Such fragile items could only be looked at and admired. We made a deal that we would not pick them up, because it had taken us a long time to create them, and our time would have been wasted if we played with them and broke them. From that day on, I have been observant and have trained my eyes to admire beauty and my hands to resist touching delicate objects. This is what I learned that many artists develop over the years. Close observation is a type of discipline for the eye, and I was on the journey toward becoming a master at it.

When my family visited the supermarket, I always asked to go to the ice cream section. We would agree on the ice cream flavor and there it went, into the metal carriage along with the other grocery items. On one particular day, when everyone had finished eating supper, we all wanted an ice cream bar. Upon finishing my ice cream, I was left with the wooden stick in my hands. I would eat every bit of chocolate until the stick was spotless. I was bored, and went into the kitchen and rinsed off all the brown color from the chocolate covering. While rinsing the stick, I thought, what can I use this for? Should I put the stick in the trash or dry it and use it for something? I put the wooden stick on a napkin to let it dry. In my bedroom, I got a piece of paper and a pencil, and started to draw. I had learned in school to create squares, triangles, and circles, and to make a design using those shapes. I thought about using the shapes I had learned without too much change to the stick. I drew a box, then a lid, and then several designs. Finally, I had created a design on the paper.

I saw that I had designed a box on a piece of paper without any extreme effort. It felt as though the paper had been expecting the drawing to appear. When my family had finished eating their ice cream bars, I asked them to save their sticks for me. I washed all the sticks and dried them. After several days, I had collected a hand full of sticks for my next project. When the wooden sticks were dry, I looked in my bedroom for the white glue and began gluing the sticks together, piece by piece, until what I had created resembled the design from the paper. My urge to finish the art project was consuming my every thought and as my project came to its final stage, I felt a sense of accomplishment. When I finished the piece of artwork—an improvised wooden stick box—I was already thinking of my next art creation.

My ice cream stick art idea had grown stronger. Ideas flowed in my head of what to create with the sticks. I asked my parents to buy ice cream bars on a regular basis, to the point where I was annoying them with the ice cream issue. Then one day, on another visit to the supermarket, I walked toward the ice cream section and saw a display of kitchen items. On the bottom shelf were many white boxes with tiny writing on them. I could barely see the writing or understand what it said. One of the boxes was open and had many ice cream sticks in it. This brought a huge smile to my face. I never knew that clean, ready-to-use sticks were available at the supermarket. These were probably for people who made homemade ice cream bars or pastries requiring something to hold them with. I didn't know exactly what these sticks were used for, but that didn't stop me from continuing with my reason to have them. I ran to my parents and asked them to buy me a box of sticks instead of ice cream bars. They agreed with my request, and I was one happy little boy.

At home, I created a large box; then I added a top, then a second box on top of the original one. My idea was to create a wooden house resembling those of Spanish architecture found in San Juan. The Spanish houses had second and third floors with balconies. I recalled seeing the houses all close together when we had visited the *Viejo San Juan*[7] area. The balconies had metal railings with plants hanging from them. The light fixtures were old, rusty metal boxes hanging from the side of the houses, usually close to the doors or on the corners. Some of these lamps were lit by gas and others by electricity. I wanted to create a work of art that took me back to the old neighborhoods of the *Viejo San Juan* in Puerto Rico.

Every day after school, I dedicated time to my new wooden house. It took me about a week or so, due to the time that I had to wait for the glue to dry after each session. After I had created the structure, I painted it brown to help make the side panels look like old wood. I added items that gave it a unique resemblance to the old-fashioned Spanish colonial houses. It had a balcony all around the top floor. The bottom section was a small restaurant. And since my father worked with electrical parts, he had pieces of wire around the house that I could use. I added electrical and mechanical parts to enhance my creation.

The tools I used sometimes came from his old toolbox, which had a strange odor. He had to oil his metal tools in order to keep them from rusting, and in the enclosed space of the metal box, this created a unique odor. I used his soldering tool and lead to connect metal pieces. I connected small lights to a switch device that illuminated the interior of the bottom floor, and I attached the wires to a small battery in the back. I made a small mop from white string, and a broomstick and the top railings from shish kebab skewers. The Spanish-style house was coming to its full realization. I was proud of myself for doing something different and unique.

I put my new creation away in my room where no one could tamper with it. I only took it out to show my family members, and would always put it back in my room to safeguard it. Every other weekend, our neighbor's family would come visit her. Our neighbor, Doña Benita, was an older lady with white hair. She lived alone and rarely left her house. On one of those visits, her daughter-in-law was intrigued when I showed her my artwork. This cheerful and lovely lady's name was Idalia. She soon fell in love with what I had created. I was so happy that she saw the potential of a great artist in me. I hadn't realized that it was unusual to have a great imagination and to transform ideas into real-life creations.

Idalia was a kind, loving, good-humored woman. She saw so much potential in my artwork that she proposed that I create more houses, ones that actually could hang from the wall. The houses she mentioned needed to be easily carried and handled without being damaged. I was curious as to why they had to be as she indicated. She explained that she would be able to sell them for me, and would give me all the proceeds to purchase more materials. I was so happy with her idea that soon after her visit I ran to the store and purchased another box of sticks and more glue. At home, I drew and created different styles, to offer variety to the potential buyers. When I exhausted that idea, I went outside and drew the facades, or the front sections, of each house on our street. Those were enough sketches to keep me busy for the weeks I had to wait until her next visit.

Every day after school, I found myself gluing sticks together and adding a rope on the back to hang the house when it was finished. I also painted the houses different colors to give variety to my work. The night before Idalia's next visit, I put the houses I created into sandwich bags in order to keep the bright colors from getting dirty. The bags also protected them from dust and water. The next morning, I was happy to wait for Idalia, her husband Ruben and their daughter Jessica. Their blue and white 1980 Ford Thunderbird made a distinct noise that was created by the steering system. Every time Ruben moved the steering wheel, the car made a squeaking loud noise. I had gotten used to hearing the particular sound of their car. When they arrived, I ran to my room and collected all the artworks, put them in a box, and went outside.

When I went to our neighbor's house, I saw a big smile on Idalia's face. I had done what she had told me. I had created around fifteen different styles of houses in various colors and with unique attachments. She said that I would one day be a good businessman. I was not looking to become a businessman—I was interested in becoming an artist. Little did I know that I was already an artist. She had the talent to persuade people to buy art and I had the talent to create it. I saw us as improvised mobile art dealers. From that moment on, I never saw her as a businesswoman, but as a loving and caring second mom who believed in me and my talent. She treated me like her own son, and has always been a great influence in my life. She cared for my studies, art projects, and school grades. Her influence helped me improve academically and artistically during my schooling. She continues to be a dear woman in my life, and I will never forget her for being such an influential person in my childhood years. I learned that my art was a calling and that I was here to create it from the heart. I used the money she gathered to purchase more art materials and to continue my journey in creating art and expressing my artistic side. I still have and treasure the first house I ever created using ice cream bar sticks.

"The animals had taught me to be responsible by caring for them."

GRANDPA AT AGE TWELVE

I remember the first day of school when I began the sixth grade. The first thing my teacher asked me was if I was Luis Angel and Meicy's son. I looked at her in a shockingly surprised fashion—she just had mentioned the names of my parents. She told me that I had my father's facial features and that my nose would not hide his name. I was then concerned about anything I did for the rest of the school year. My teacher had gone to school with my parents. Cidra is a small town in Puerto Rico and everyone knew each other. I knew that she could always call my parents if I misbehaved. In spite of her being so strict in the classroom, I later came to enjoy her class.

Around the holidays, my teacher taught us many songs that had been made popular by various popular singers. Among them was the Italian singer Tony Croatto, who moved to the island and began singing Puerto Rican folk music. Another great singer was Danny Rivera, who to this day I still listen to and enjoy during the festive season. Jose Feliciano is another great singer and songwriter, who made his famous song *Feliz Navidad*[8] a classic Christmas pop song.

The songs were inspiring and made the holidays a joyful time. I remember the songs being on the local radio stations every holiday from then on.

One day while walking home from school, I passed by the pet store located at the corner of Jose de Diego Street and

Tomas Maestre Street. My grandma's house was the forth house up on Tomas Maestre. The streets are so small I was at the pet shop within two minutes. I stared at the animals, wanting to touch each and every one of them. I enjoyed looking at the large bird with the long red tail and blue chest with yellow stripes. I had no idea what type of bird this was. Inside, I stared at that large bird for a long time. It was not inside of a cage but was instead perched on a thick wooden dowel above a large tray, eating peanuts and staring at me. I stared back at the impressive bird as it took a peanut shell, cracked it open, and ate the contents. The shopkeeper approached me and asked if I was looking for a particular kind of pet. I inquired about the name of the bird and she responded that its name was Charlie. I asked her if all birds like it were called Charlie. She said no, the bird was of the *guacamayo*[9] species and she had named it Charlie. She stated that this particular bird was not for sale. I told her that I enjoyed animals and that I would like to have them all. She laughed and told me that it would be impossible to care for so many animals in one's home. She asked me again if I was interested in a particular pet. I told her that it had to be a pet that made little noise because I did not want to upset anyone at home.

I already had fish, a cat, a turtle, hamsters, and now I wanted a bird. I had to make sure that the animals did not wake anyone up at night or bother them during the day. I remember my father got upset because the fish tank pump made noise in the living room. He told me to put it in my room after that. The lady at the shop told me that having one bird would not be a good idea because it would get lonely by itself. She asked me how much money I had to spend. I told her I had not counted my savings yet. Then she told me if I wanted a bird, I would need a cage, food, and water to provide for its care. I told her I would think about it and return the next day.

I ran home and opened my piggy bank. I counted all the change and it added up to around $12.50. The next day, I woke up a little earlier than usual and ran to the pet store. The pet store was only one block away from my house. The doors were closed and I saw the sign with the hours of business posted. It read 9:00 a.m.—6:00 p.m. I figured it was too early to be there, so I walked to school. I was thinking all day that I would have a new pet that afternoon. I really wanted that one bird as a pet, but I knew it was not for sale. The school day seemed so short, and after it ended and the school bell rang, I ran to the pet store. I rushed to the pet keeper and told her that I had $12.50 to spend. She laughed and told me that I had enough to buy one bird. She also asked if I had a cage for the bird. I told her no, but I would make one. There was chicken wire in the yard and I could use it. The woman told me that chicken wire had large openings and small birds could escape. I said that I had caught birds in my backyard with a cage I made. She opened her eyes wide as if she was surprised. I told her that I created a box-style cage with an opening on the bottom. I described how I had caught wild birds by placing sugar on the ground, tying a thin rope to a stick, and then placing the stick between the cage and the ground. I would wait patiently until the birds began eating the sugar, and then I would pull the string. That's how I trapped the birds. When my grandma had seen me doing this, she had been upset and told me that wild birds could not live in captivity for a long time in small cages. She told me to set them free.

The kind lady at the store proceeded to make me a deal. I felt like a grown up and tried to act as such, but it was obvious I was no businessman, and of course I was only twelve years old. She told me that I did not have enough money to purchase the two birds we had spoken about, let alone a cage and bird food. I felt a little sad and discouraged. She told me to think about what I was doing. She made a deal to sell me only the cage, at a lower price. All my money went to the cage. So, I walked home that afternoon with a wooden bird cage and no birds, but I was so content because I was one step closer to having my birds. I wanted birds as pets because I saw my neighbor's balcony full of parakeets in a cage. The entire street can hear the birds chirping every morning.

My parents were working, and as usual my Grandma Luisa was waiting for me in the living room looking out the screen door. When I arrived home, my grandma told me that she had gone to put some change in my piggy bank and had found that it was completely empty. When she saw the cage in my hands, she figured out what I had done. She said that she would tell my father that she had purchased the cage for me so that I would not get in trouble. She told me there was no place to put the cage, and that having birds would bring unnecessary noise into the house. My grandma was always complacent, and she usually agreed with my choices. I felt so happy because she understood how badly I wanted pet birds. I loved my grandma very much because she always showed her unconditional love for me. She saw how happy animals made me feel. I told her that I would save all my money to buy the birds.

The next morning, she woke me up and told me to get ready for school. I could smell the aroma from the coffee she made. I had a routine in the mornings. I woke up, ran to the bathroom, and did my regular hygiene procedures. By the time came into the dining room, out she had breakfast on the table. There was nothing better than homemade grandma-style scrambled eggs, toast, and a glass of orange juice. Before leaving the house, I gave my grandma a kiss and said *bendición*.[10]

That morning, the day after I had purchased the birdcage, my grandma said, "I have a surprise for you before you leave for school." That put a big smile on my face. She went to her room and came back. Her right hand was closed, and with her left hand she grabbed my right hand and put a twenty-dollar bill in it. I looked at her and asked what the money was for. She replied by saying, "Buy your birds and the food for them, and bring back the change." I gave her a big hug and kiss and said, "Thank you, *Abuela*."[11] I walked to school so happy, with a big smile on my face. I was talking to myself all day. Other students looked at me like I was crazy. I didn't care what other people said. I just knew that I was going to buy the two birds I so wanted.

After school, I ran to the pet store and rushed inside to find the lady who cared for the animals. She greeted me by saying, "You're back! And you seem happy, too. How can I help you, little one?" I told her that I had the money to purchase the birds. She asked, "What kind of bird?" I told her one like Charlie. "Charlie is not for sale," she reminded me, "and that kind of bird costs thousands of dollars."

"What kind of bird can I buy?" I asked.
"How much do you have?"

"Twenty dollars."

The lady looked at me very seriously and said, "Where are you getting so much money?" I told her that my grandma had given me the money to get the birds I wanted.

"Well, well, well," she said. "With that money you can only buy either a pair of parakeets or a pair of finches." The kind lady indicated that the wooden cage that I had purchased the day before would not be an appropriate home for parakeets because they would chew on the wooden dowels and escape. Therefore, the finches were the perfect birds to live in the wooden cage. So, there I was, picking the colors of the birds that would go home with me. She gave me a bag of seed and put a pair of finches inside a small cardboard box, with holes so they could breath. The box had animal designs printed on the sides. She told me that the box was good enough until I got home, and that finches made less noise compared to parakeets.

I wanted to run home to show my grandma, but I went as slow as I could in order to not disturb my new friends. When I got home, I opened the wooden cage and let the birds in. I placed the cage in the dining room side table. I went to tell my grandma that I was home, and I gave her the few dollars of the change. She wanted to see the birds as much as I wanted to show her. She enjoyed seeing the birds fly inside their new home. The male was white with orange-colored cheeks and the female was completely gray. The finches made a low chirping sound, not so loud as to disturb our family or the neighbors. On that day, I learned that birds brought a new spirit of joy into a house. Several days later I placed a nest I purchased at the pet store so they could sleep comfortable. The finches never stayed in one location for a long time, only when they were in their nest. Their energy was contagious, and even their chirping was a song of joy. Each day, I came home from school and sat in front of the cage for hours, just staring at the birds. When the wild birds sang from outside the window, the finches sang and jumped as if they wanted to fly to freedom.

Several weeks passed and the birds were as happy as usual. I recall that one day after school, my grandma said to me, "You are a grandpa."

I stared at her with a strange look and asked her to repeat what she had said. I was confused, because I had learned that grandfathers were older people, usually with white hair and wiser than me.

She said, "Congratulations, you have become a grandfather at age twelve." I laughed and she then said that the finches had laid several eggs. I told her that I'd never looked inside the nest to see if they had eggs. She was as happy as I was. She told me that nature was calling the birds back, and when the little ones hatched and grew into adults, it would be time for them to see freedom and embrace Mother Nature. She also said that the new ones and their parents would outgrow the cage and that it wouldn't be fair to keep so many birds in one cage. I then learned, just as my grandma had said, that grandparents let their offspring go free after they have taken good care of them. When children become adults they are old enough to live on their own. She said that's what grandparents do; take care of the children until they are old enough to see the world on their own. I didn't understand her then, but today I recognize what her dear heart was telling me. At the age of twelve, I began to see in myself the traits of a caring grandfather.

My childhood pets taught me to be responsible by caring for them. And even though my parents allowed me to have so many animals, it was still my responsibility to care for them. I made sure they had fresh water, fresh air from the windows, and proper food. It saddened me that when the baby finches were old enough, I would have to let them fly into freedom. Because I was so attached to my birds and happy when I saw the new birds had hatched. There little bodies were completely bare with no feathers. They looked so defenseless that I decided to keep all of them.

I made a large cage where they would have more room to fly and enjoy each other's company. I then learned from the pet store keeper that animals raised in captivity often cannot survive in the wild after being provided with food and shelter their entire lives. I was scared that if I set them free they would die of hunger. My grandmother agreed, and always reminded me to change the water daily, clean the cage, and have seeds available for all the birds. She also reminded me that sweeping up the mess they made when the seeds fell onto the floor and cleaning their cage was my responsibility. I was only twelve years old, but in that small, important way, I was already a grandpa. When the baby finches became adults, I placed the new metal cage outside of my bedroom window so I could see and hear them. I saw other wild birds eating the seeds that fell out of the cage. It brought a big smile to my face when I saw the finches had made new friends that eventually visited them everyday.

"One does not know what one has until it is taken away."

THE PERFECT STORM

It was a humid late afternoon, and the birds in the sky gathered in groups, making themselves heard and acknowledged by the people below. It seemed that they were giving signs and warnings to the people that something was about to happen. The sky was cloudy, yet not enough to block the sun on the horizon. The wind had thickened, to the point that one could barely breathe normally. The people on the streets trotted along, clutching their garments, groceries, and umbrellas as if they were going to be grabbed by an unwanted stranger. I could hear the dogs in the neighborhood barking and cars making squeaky noises. I saw the people covering up windows with tape and acting as if something was going to happen.

It was the fall of 1989 and I was thirteen years old. I was known by many people as one who was serious, observant, and curious. I was observant of my surroundings and curious to investigate the unknown. Like many teenagers, I wanted to be, act, and talk like I was older. My voice changed; it got deeper, more adult-sounding. I no longer had the childish voice of a little boy. I didn't notice the change in my voice until my cousin Jacqueline told me. She surely was one to point out one's flaws. From that moment on, I realized that the people in my life expected me to act like an adult. I guess my voice had convinced people of that idea.

That summer, my family often gathered with close family members who lived an hour from our house. We sometimes stayed with our extended family on the weekends to experience some great family time. I didn't watch too much television due to my adventurous way of exploring the outdoors, primarily our backyard. When it was time to go to my aunt's house, I unexpectedly was caught doing something else and was told to pack some clothes, as we would be heading out soon. I never packed excessively. Most of the time, our family would gather at Luquillo Beach for picnics and barbeques. This beach has a line of *Kioskos* filled with lots of traditional homemade foods of the island. Luquillo Beach is one of the most famous and visited beach of the islanders. Among the many traditional foods found there are the *pinchos*, *alcapurrias*, *bacalaitos*, and *mofongo*. Among the drinks were *agua de coco*, malta India, sodas, and natural homemade juices. Those were good old times that I will never forget. When the family got together it was like being at a party. There was food, laughter, games, and time to relax and enjoy the moment. I really enjoyed the beach, feeling the warm sand under my bare feet and smelling the salt from the sea. On this particular Sunday the air seemed different. It had a peculiar smell and I had a strange feeling something was not right. It seemed as if the winds spoke in a low voice from afar. The *changos* sang loudly, which made them seem close, although they were on the electrical pole lines at a distance, some flew low over the houses, as if announcing the arrival of a storm. It was indeed a signal that something in the atmosphere was alerting them too. The dogs' senses were alerted by these hovering creatures that came and went as they pleased. The barking of the dogs made me wonder whether something was about to happen. When night came calling, there was barely a glimmer of light from the sky illuminating the streets. The streetlights covered the rough black asphalt of those small, irregular city streets. The temperature and velocity of the winds became unpredictable. At one moment there was little wind, and the next moment it could pick you up off the ground. Late into the night, I felt unsettled in my bed, unable to rid myself of a strange, unusual feeling, but finally I did fall asleep just thinking the night away.

My aunt, uncle, and cousin were awake early the next morning. They were watching television, and surprisingly there was no one outside. They usually opened the side door to let the air come in, but that morning it was wise not to. The newscast announced that a hurricane was about to hit the northeastern section of Puerto Rico. My aunt gathered batteries and a small black radio, pots and pans, and closed all the windows. The winds were fast and irregular. The street was silent, but the winds were not yet powerful enough to lift cars or cause massive destruction, as the television anchorman was describing. My aunt, cousin, and I filled pots and pans with water. We searched the house for every available container, filling each with fresh tap water, including mop pails, the washing machine, and the bathtub. It was said that on the island the water was restricted and even not available for periods of hours and even days after a storm. At one point, I heard it was because the lakes that provided water to the cities and small towns were drying up and water needed to be used wisely. When there was no water available in the past and the faucets released only air, we all knew about the problem on the news. Conservation of water was asked and people got use to the limited resources. Having water saved in containers gave us some sort of comfort, even if we didn't have to use it.

I could not figure out why the people on the television were showing scenes from past storms. They were rating which storm was stronger and the dates they had occurred. To me, it was not the time for statistics and information on storms that had occurred at the beginning of the 1900's, let alone things that had vanished because of them. In my opinion, it might have been to scare people and make them terrified to step outside their front doors. I never had experienced so much uncertainty and fear similar to the one that day. Sensing fear because of the anchorman's exaggerations was a story of its own.

The wind made strange noises, like someone whispering nonsense in your ear. The noise came through the cracks around the doors and windows. The windows consisted of horizontal, interlocking aluminum flaps that tapped against each other by the wind. We expected to lose all forms of contact with family and the outside world. It was known in the past that the electricity would cease for hours at a time throughout the island even when a storm had not paid us a visit. Now, because of the huge storm, we were in for a surprise.

I knew the phone lines were still working because I heard the phone ring. It was my brother, indicating that he would come over soon to help with last-minute preparations. I thought he was crazy for risking his life, but the storm hadn't quite arrived yet. Ten minutes later we heard a horn outside; it was my father in his beige, late 1970s two-door Pinto station wagon, dropping my brother off. When I ran to the balcony, I could see my brother getting out of the Pinto. He ran upstairs as my father drove off. I considered myself brave, but my brother was the brave one that day. It was close to 8:30 a.m., and the wind had picked up tremendously. We could hear the roof making grinding noises, as if it might rip away from above us. My uncle and aunt owned a two-family home on Eider Street. They rented the first floor and lived on the second floor.

The first floor had belonged to my aunt's parents for many years before they built the second floor. The second floor was cooler because the normally calm breezes weren't blocked by the neighboring houses. I overheard my aunt and uncle talking about the construction of the house and their worries of possible structural damage. The first floor was completely constructed of cement, including the roof. The second floor was constructed of cement except for the roof, which was made of galvanized aluminum. It was light enough to not cause structural damage or exert excess weight upon the first floor. Because of its light weight and flexibility, the possibility of the storm winds lifting up the roof concerned my aunt and uncle and the entire family. Two metal tension ropes had been installed years prior in order to help protect the roof from bad winds, but only the center portions were protected. This condition left all four corners of the house vulnerable to the storm's strong winds.

The winds picked up tremendously, reaching close to 100 mph. The phone lines went out, the electricity vanished, and all we heard was the news on the small battery-operated radio and the wind. It was Monday morning, September 18, 1989, when the eye of Hurricane Hugo struck the northeastern part of the island. Although we were not at that part of the island, we sure felt like it. It was still morning, around 10 o'clock, when the winds reached full strength and made themselves known. Everyone in the house was scared and nervous. The roof was in danger of being ripped off above our heads. We all heard a loud banging in the back of the house from the direction of Jessica's bedroom. Water and wind were coming from the top corner of the ceiling. Her room was decorated with Strawberry Shortcake designs and dolls everywhere. Her bed had a canopy with the same designs on it. She had her books, toys, and clothes neatly placed. She was three years younger than me. The metal roof, loosened by the angry winds, flapped up and down, and I thought it might unroll like an old carpet and detach itself from the house. I saw my aunt praying, and my uncle looked terrified.

My uncle quickly went to get wire and tools from the hallway closet. My brother, uncle, and I went outside to tie down the corners of the roof, to keep it from flapping up and letting more wind lift other sections. It was a very stressful moment for all of us. When we all went outside, the winds were so strong that we had to grab onto the walls and stay close together so we wouldn't fly away. We walked close to the wall until we reached the corner of the house. One interesting part made this ordeal challenging. There were metal railings dividing the sections of the patio and the corner of the roof. Due to the railings protected us from large flying objects, such as metal pieces from other roofs, chicken cages, and tree branches. The railings we were safe, but because of the openings, the winds were still a factor in the problem. My uncle gave us the instructions. My brother was the brave one to get up and tie a rope and wire to hold down the corner of the flapping metal. I provided the tools as he needed them. After thirty minutes of struggling with the wind and battling our fears, the mission was completed and the corner was safe. My brother was the hero, and thanks to him the roof did not suffer more damage. My aunt was praying that no other corner would come loose and fly away.

That morning the minutes felt like hours and the hours felt like days. It was the longest period of time that I had ever been under so much fear and stress. We didn't know if the storm was in its resting time and would come back. My uncle told me that if we were under the eye of the hurricane, the next part of the storm that was coming could be worse. During the late afternoon the sky was clearing, yet still cloudy, with no rain. There was still tension among everyone in the house. The wind slowed and everyone emerged from their homes. Outside it looked like a war zone. Light poles had been knocked down, street wires lay on the ground, and the road was littered with fallen trees, branches, and scraps of metal. No one mentioned it, but it was clean-up time. Because there was no electricity or water, I was thinking no television and no showers. Neighbors began talking to each other, making sure everyone was alive and safe.

We went into the backyard of the house and found all of the fruit on the ground. There was a mango tree, several banana trees, and an avocado tree from the back side property that had half of the tree branches on our side. The neighbors had chickens and roosters inside large metal cages. The cages had been opened by the strong winds, and the roofs of the cages were no longer there. The chickens and roosters were loose running around both properties. Nearly all of the avocados from the neighbor's tree were on our side of the fence. While cleaning up the mess, we picked up all the fruit and put it inside the house. I was happy about the avocadoes because they were my favorite. I was not a fan of the mangoes. Surprisingly, the neighbor was not around, and probably didn't know that her cages were open and the animals were loose. She was not one to share the crops of her tree. Even with the branches of the avocado tree hanging on my family's property, she still would not have liked the fact that someone was taking her avocados.

Night was approaching and my uncle and aunt wanted to see my aunt's sister.

Since there was no electricity or phone service, we all wanted to be together. My aunt grabbed several bags of our clothes and other items. My uncle went back to the backyard and we all followed him. He started chasing the chickens. My uncle caught a chicken and put it in a sack, which he placed into the trunk of the car, and off we went to my aunt's sister's house. All of my family was together, talking about the experience of the storm. We went to Manuela's house where we all gathered and stayed for several days. Ruben, Idalia, Jessica, Sara, Geraldo, Tito, Isabel, Luis, my father and I were having the best time of our lives. There was no electricity or running water available in the neighborhood. On the radio, it was announced that 75 percent of the island had no electricity due to hurricane damage. That evening, the chicken found in my uncle's backyard was boiling in a kitchen pot, seasoned and being cooked for that day's supper.

Due to my past experiences, I am a true believer in not hurting animals. I had learned that animals share the same space we do and have a mission on earth. At times they eat each other, and sooner or later some are eaten by humans.

Due to the hardship of my family, I understood that eating a chicken was not a sin, but that night I passed on my part of the chicken. I was too conscious of eating an animal I had once seen alive. Some of my family members told me that in the past, many people had done the same in times of hardship. I had once seen how a pig was prepared for dinner. It was not a lovely scene. The people preparing the pigs in the *lechonera*[12] seemed heartless. The intenstines of the pig are cleaned, filled with blood and rice, cooked and eaten. The ears, feet, and tail are eaten in homemade stew. I believe every single part of the pig is cooked and eaten in some fancy delicacy dish.

After experiencing how *morcillas*[13] were made for the holidays, I learned to pass on it. I no longer eat *morcillas* because of the experience of watching how it's prepared. On the island, eating pork is a holiday tradition, along with rice, *gandules*,[14] and salad. *Coquito*[15] and *ponche*[16] are favorite holiday drinks not to forget.

A day had passed, and not having access to supermarkets troubled me. The ice was expensive and food became difficult to find. Our stove used gas, so not having electricity did not deter us from having a warm meal. Our neighbors took turns heading out to the river for water. After boiling, it was safe to drink. I enjoyed the warm water in the shower and was often reminded to save some for the others. But not having electricity caused us to revert to ancient times. My brother had stuffed a shirt into the roof's drainpipe. Because the roof was flat and had cinder blocks all around it, water could be trapped. This became the family's shower system until water service was restored to the neighborhood. It was a little embarrassing to be semi-naked outside, but the feeling of having water to bathe in was worth the effort and shame.

The storm experience was one that I came to cherish over time. Although our family, friends, and neighbors experienced needing the basics that normally made us comfortable, we all enjoyed the quality time together. One does not know what one has until it is taken away. Our family experienced much quality time in the aftermath of that hurricane, telling stories, making jokes, and bonding with one another. Although the storm had taken away water, electricity, and some of my time off from school, I enjoyed every minute spent with my family, friends, and neighbors. Several weeks later, I wrote about these experiences for a school assignment. My story was similar to those of other classmates, except that several were still without the basic home necessities. They explained that they were still suffering, even though several weeks had passed. The storm had caused several deaths, including people drowning and workers getting electrocuted trying to return power to the neighborhoods. Even though the storm caused chaos among family, friends, and the community, it brought us all together, like it always should be. I learned then that quality time is more important than the quantity of time. The several weeks I spent with my family during Hurricane Hugo will always remain in my memory, and I will never forget how one scary storm made my family cherish and love each other even more. I also learned that material things really don't matter when you have your loved ones around. There is nothing that will ever replace the love of family and friends.

"The principle of being honest was ingrained in me by my experience."

THE COST OF TWENTY DOLLARS

It was a humid afternoon on a spring day when the phone rang. As children, we were not allowed to answer it. My grandmother's sister, Mama Gume, picked it up and spoke for a while. Recognizing that the call was not for us, we continued playing. After school, my brother and I liked to play *gallito*[17] and *trompo*[18] on the driveway. Before there was even the thought of having electronic pocket-sized devices to play with, there was the game of *gallito*. The material used for the *gallito* game is a hard bean found inside an *algarroba*.[19] Inside the hard, thick-shelled *algarroba* is a yellow powdery and edible substance that has a strong odor similar to rotten eggs. When the *algarroba* is taken from the tree, it's cracked open and the largest beans are taken out and cleaned. The beans are hard and difficult to break.

After the beans are cleaned, a hole is made in the middle to tie a piece of string about a foot or so long. The game is usually for two, but others can play at the same time. One player lays down his or her bean and the other person tries to break it with the other bean, and the game continues until one bean is broken. The first person to break the other's bean wins the game. In order to do this one lays a bean down and the other person slaps the bean with all his force using the sting and force to weaken it. My brother and I learned this game when we were in third grade. There was a large *algarroba* tree on the school grounds. All of the kids would climb the tree and take an algarroba. No one would want to open it due to its strong, bad odor. When all the boys got together, they collected their lunch money and gave it to the bravest one, who would open the *algarroba*, remove the seeds, and eat part of the yellow powdery contents. After the brave one ate the contents and took out all the beans, he was paid. My brother and I took our lunches to school, so we didn't have as much money as the other students. We had enough to buy one or two beans from the other students. The beans were about an inch wide and as thick as a coffee bean. The game is fun and convenient for kids. You can put the bean in any pocket and go about your business.

My brother and I shared the same room at home. The pair of bunk beds allowed us enough floor space to walk around. I slept on the top and he slept on the bottom. There was a closet big enough to walk inside. On the edge of the wooden doors we both made marks to see who was taller. We did this every day until we got bored with it. My brother, Luis, is one year and fourteen days older than me. But I was as tall as he was and many people thought we were twins. We dressed the same for school because it was mandatory to wear a uniform.

One Friday morning, my aunt paid a visit to our school to ask the teachers about homework. She asked why I got homework and my brother didn't. His teacher told her that she didn't believe in homework, and that all schoolwork needed to be completed in school. I thought my brother was lucky for having such a cool teacher. His teacher was soft-spoken and very nice to the students, but my teacher was grumpy and had a bad temper.

In school, I remember the ceilings being about twenty feet high, with windows that ran up to them. The ceiling fans had sharp metal blades similar to airplane propellers. There were two doors in the classroom. One door was the entrance from the hallway and the other door led to the schoolyard. The doors were thick, wooden, castle-like doors that locked with a wooden piece across the middle from the inside and with a padlock on the outside. Because there were no window screens, birds often paid us a visit and interrupted class. There was no way of stopping the traffic of birds into the classroom because both the doors and the windows were open.

I wanted to be in my brother's class because they had fish tanks in the room. My teacher was so strict. Her demeanor scared me and I felt uncomfortable being in her classroom. I often looked out the windows and daydreamed for minutes, which at times felt like hours. I prayed for recess and lunchtime to arrive so that I could go outside and play with my friends. My teacher was mean to the students, but I couldn't tell my parents because according to them the teacher always was right. I remember many students had to participate and go to the front of the class to read from the board. On one occasion, a girl was called and didn't feel comfortable reading in front of the class. The teacher screamed at her and demanded that she go in front of the class or she would call the girl's parents after school. The girl was chubby, with long shiny black hair and thick black-framed glasses. She was intelligent, but also shy. Several other students were called to stand at the board in front of the class. Lucky me, I wasn't called to stand up there. I was also shy and nervous in front of my classmates. I was scared that I wouldn't know the answer to her question or the practice exercise on the board. I will never forget the moment when I heard everyone making loud noises and laughing. I was easily distracted, looking out the windows, playing with my eraser, and drawing small sketches in my notebook. I looked up to see the students standing in front of the class, and the others sitting at their desks pointing their fingers at the girl with the thick black-framed glasses. I was amazed by what I saw at that moment.

My heart pounded harder and harder as the students laughed loudly. Then, there was complete silence in the room when the teacher ordered everyone to quiet down. The chubby girl standing up started crying as a wet stain appeared below her waistline. The wet stain started small but grew bigger and bigger. She put her hands over her face as she cried in front of the class. The tops of her shoes were wet and her socks were soaked. The school uniform for girls was a checkered vest and a skirt cut below the knee. She had urinated on herself because she was so scared of standing in front and speaking to the class.

I never felt the same about my teacher again. I was sweating and nervous, thinking that I would be called next. But then she told us to sit at our desks and continue silently on our own. The day continued like that, with little noise. All I heard was the pages of the students' notebooks turning. The girl who had peed on herself was sent to the office so that her parents could pick her up from school. I wanted so badly to tell another adult that the teacher had caused the girl such embarrassment. Every student in the class had humiliated her and made fun of her. I felt so bad that I couldn't help what had happened to another student. I sensed that the teacher had her own problems that we little ones could not understand at the time. The teacher was older, strict, and exhibited a mean demeanor. But when another teacher or a parent arrived at the door, her personality changed drastically, like she was the sweetest person on earth.

Another incident concerned one of the boys who sat next to me. He was serious, quiet, and shy, and I could relate to him because I was the same way. By shy, I mean the students that were not outspoken and did not yell when they talked to me or to others. I recognized that he was artistic because all of his written assignments were written in calligraphy. His writing was fancy, delicate, and appealing to an artistic eye.

What happened to him has never left my memory. The teacher usually walked around to every student's desk to see if he or she was on task. Her desk was at the back of the classroom, behind the students. All of the students faced the chalkboard. The teacher would remain at her desk and could see what everyone was doing. We could never see when she was looking at us because we all had our backs to her. There were four rows, and I was in one of the last of them. I could not hear her walking toward me, because in the mornings when she opened the classroom door she would have on high heels, but as soon as she sat at her desk, she took them off and put on low-heeled soft shoes that made no noise when she walked around. I knew she was doing it for a reason.

During her routine visits to the students' desks, she stopped at the desk of the boy beside me. He seemed afraid to look her in the eye. He always looked at the floor when she spoke to him. We were learning to write in cursive and she noticed his fancy writing. This may have required him to write slowly as well. She would usually tell students to look at their own work and not at anyone else's. What my eyes saw was shocking and disturbing.

While she was at the desk next to mine, she screamed at the student in his ear for writing slowly. She wanted him to write faster and with a less distinctive design. She continued screaming in his ear, twisted and pulled on his ears, pulled his hair, and hit him on his knuckles several times with a ruler. I saw how the tears ran down his face. He was silent and his face was red. She looked at me, and told me to mind my own business and to look the other way. I asked the girl beside me if she had seen the same thing I did, since I had seen her glance at the ordeal right along with me.

After five minutes, the girl stood up and went to the teacher. When the girl returned to her desk, the teacher came up to me, pulled on my sideburns, smacked my knuckles with the ruler, and told me that if I had a comment to make, to tell her directly to her face. I looked at the girl, who smiled and looked the other way. I instantly decided that the girl had lied to the teacher, and told her that I had made a comment about her treating a student badly in class. I guess the girl had read my mind, because that was not exactly what I asked her. The only thing I asked the girl was if she had seen the same thing I'd seen.

To this day I think the teacher was guilty. I later learned that the girl was the teacher's pet. The girl was the teacher's second pair of eyes and ears. I then started mistrusting people for lying to others. I let the feelings of the incident go and it was gone with the wind. I never talked to the lying girl again and I avoided interacting with her. I never told anyone about what the teacher had done during these shocking moments in class. I didn't think anyone would believe me. I kept quiet, reserved, and careful of what I told others.

I enjoyed my time in the schoolyard, however. My friends would play *gallito* during lunchtime and climb the trees. I remember a beautiful girl, Rosa, in my brother's class. Her mom would come during lunchtime to sit with her and play in the yard. Because I was so fascinated with this girl, I would stare at her. She would jump rope with the other girls while her mom held one side of the rope. They would take turns jumping. I could only look from afar, because the boys stayed on one side of the yard and the girls on the other. We kind of had our own gender ruled games. I would catch her looking at me when her mom was occupied and attending to her friends. She would look at me and smile, and that meant the world to me. This was my first crush.

That was really the main reason, along with playing with my friends, to have lunch and be outside. On one of those hot afternoons, during the bus ride home, I wondered what could I do to impress this girl. I had to do something to make her want to be with me. I was determined and thought hard, but nothing came to mind. When I got home, I went to my room, took off my shoes, and lay on my bed for a while thinking of her.

I recalled that my grandma's sister had asked me to get a pair of scissors from her room. She usually sat in the enclosed balcony in her rocking chair, knitting away and creating designs. She would spend hours rocking in her chair, knitting, and watching television, all at the same time. She sent me to her room and off I went. I was told to look for something on her dresser. The off-white antique Victorian dresser had a mirror on the back and a clear glass cover over the wood, probably to protect the wood from her perfume bottles and makeup. It was messy and things were piled on top of each other. Lipstick, small perfume bottles, makeup compacts, several hairpins, and brushes were in the pile. Under the clear glass, there were lottery tickets, papers, and notes, and I saw a folded twenty-dollar bill. When I saw the twenty-dollar bill, I suddenly forgot what she had asked me to get in the first place. I returned to her and asked her again what exactly she wanted, and she told me to forget about it and that she would get it herself. I left it like that and returned to my room. While lying down, I was still thinking of that girl at school. Then night came and it was time for bed.

The next day at school, I paid attention to the teacher and did my work, but I still daydreamed from time to time and was still anxious for lunchtime to arrive. Once we were dismissed, my friends decided to climb the trees near the fence alongside the school. Someone had mentioned that candy was sold in the pharmacy about a block from school. One student jumped the fence, then the next, and then the next, and there I was, a fool to peer pressure, jumping the fence with the others. When I saw all the candy in the pharmacy, I was so ecstatic I had change in my pocket and bought all I could. Every one of us had a small brown bag full of candy. While I was waiting for one kid to find his money, I noticed many teddy bears on a shelf. They were white and brown colors and in many different colors. All my friends were heading out the door while I looked at the prices on the teddy bears. The kids headed back to the school and I had to catch up with them. We had to find a way to jump the school fence without anyone seeing us, but all the students were having lunch and some were playing outside. We managed to jump the fence without someone seeing us, and we all went back to the yard and began playing and sharing candy with each other. Everyone was content, because we believed no one had caught us leaving the school grounds and we all had candy in our hands.

When I got home that afternoon, I went to my room, took off my shoes, lay down on my bed, and thought about that girl at school. She had beautiful eyes, long brown hair, and a beautiful smile. When I passed my grandma's sister's bedroom, I remembered the folded twenty-dollar bill I had seen the day before under the pile of stuff. I soon found the solution to impressing the girl of my dreams. I decided to buy her one of the teddy bears I had seen at the pharmacy. I went back to the antique dresser, lifted the heavy glass, took the twenty-dollar bill, and put it in my pocket. I went to my room and hid it in my backpack.

The following day, I was in for a big adventure. I was waiting for lunchtime to go to the pharmacy with my friends to buy candy. I asked one student if he felt like getting candy and he said he didn't have any money. I said I had enough to buy for both of us. There we were, both of us jumping the fence again and heading to the pharmacy. I told him to get his candy, and I went to the teddy bear section and picked the biggest one. It was white with a red heart on it. I was so happy to have that teddy bear in my hands. I knew Rosa would like it. It meant all my love for her. My crush on her would soon be revealed. At the cash register, the attendant told me to put the teddy bear down, that the merchandise was not to be played with. I told him I was going to buy it. He asked me who it was for. I said it was for a girl at school. My friend looked at me, said I was crazy, and said there was no way I could afford to pay for it. I told him that I had enough money to pay for the teddy bear and the candy. The attendant charged me almost the entire twenty dollars.

We returned to the school and jumped the fence, and my friend went to the boys' area. I ran with the teddy bear to the girl who was on my mind. I saw her with her mother and slowed down and proceeded to go slowly towards her. We looked at each other and smiled. Her mom was smiling when I gave her the bear. The girl gave me a hug and kissed me on the cheek, and I ran off. I will never forget that moment. All of my efforts had paid off. The girl I was in love with had given me a hug. I daydreamed about it for the rest of the lunch period.

After the bell rang and all the students had returned to their classrooms, the girl's mother called my teacher to the door and spoke with her for about five minutes. I was called to the door and asked where I had gotten the money to pay for the teddy bear. The teacher told the girl's mother that I hadn't had a teddy bear that morning, and she wanted to know where I'd gotten it. The girl's mother told the teacher that she had seen me jumping the fence and coming back with the bear in my hands. I confessed that I had gotten the money from home and had not been given permission to go to the pharmacy to buy it. Soon after that, the teacher called someone from the office and I was escorted by a man who worked at the school to the pharmacy to return the teddy bear. I was so mad at my teacher, for everything she had done in the past and for making me take the teddy bear away from my love.

When I got home, I was asked if I had seen the twenty-dollar bill in my grandma's sister's bedroom. I didn't answer her and I never said yes or no. My grandma's sister seemed anxious and angry. I went to my room and fell asleep. Several hours later after my aunt, titi Elsa, got home she turned on the lights of my room. She had a belt in her hands and was slapping the leather sides against each other. She was a tall, chubby woman with dark eyes and short black hair. She looked deep into my eyes and asked me what had happened that day at school. I told her nothing had happened. She looked at me and asked if I was sure of what I was saying. She swung the belt with all her might several times, hitting me on my legs, back, and arms. I was getting the beating of my life for lying. Her mom, Mama Gume ran into the room, told her to stop what she was doing, and said that was enough. She said nothing could be reversed or changed; whatever had been done would stay in the past. I was punished by titi Elsa from that night on for several weeks. I was looked upon as a liar, a thief, and someone not to be trusted. In my mind, the only thing I had wanted to do was express my love to that sweet girl at school. No one ever cared why I had done it. They just saw that I had stolen money.

That incident taught me not to steal and to be an honest person. My life had changed in a mysterious way. After the bad beating, I never took anything that didn't belong to me, no matter what it was or how much it cost. The principle of being honest was now ingrained in me by my experience. The teacher had hit me because another student was dishonest, and I had experienced a good old-fashioned beating at home for being dishonest as well. I had learned a clear lesson. To this day, I dislike people who are not honest with me and with others. This was a life-changing experience that will never be erased from my memory. Tell the truth and you will be free from pain. Although when you speak the truth some anxieties will spark into your existence, in the long run all of your worries will be gone with the wind. I had learned that the cost of the twenty dollars I had taken without permission was much higher than I had imagined.

"Television was a means for us to relate to one another
without the outside pressures of everyday life."

SATURDAY RITUALS

On Saturday evenings, we gathered around the television set. During the week it was nearly impossible for the family to gather around the dinner table to eat due to my parents' work schedules. At first, my mom did not work and was available all the time, but then hard economic times and family problems appeared. My mother became a nurse and had different working hours. I remember her coming in late at night or early in the morning. I couldn't understand why her hours were different every week. She told me that the schedules were on a rotation and at times she was on call. I didn't know what "being on call" meant. She explained that during certain hours, she needed to be home, ready to answer the phone in case her boss called and asked her to come to work. The working schedules for nurses were 7:00 a.m.–3:00 p.m. 3:00 p.m.–11:00 p.m., and 11:00 p.m.–7:00 a.m. My mother had to work each schedule on a rotating basis. Before each shift, she assigned us chores and expected us to behave responsibly when left on our own. I was proud of my mom because she worked hard both at home and at the hospital. I missed her deeply, but I understood that she needed to work in order to make sure we could afford our household expenses.

My dad also worked, but his was a steady nine-to five job fixing electronic devices such as monitors, beepers, and other communication gadgets made by Motorola. I could say that things were not that bad. We had everything we needed, but nothing too luxurious. My mom cooked, cleaned, and cared for us to the best of her ability. Family time became difficult due to my parents' hard work outside the home.

Despite the changes, I enjoyed coming home from school each afternoon, going to the kitchen, buttering a sliced English muffin, heating it up in the toaster oven, and running to the television set. My favorite cartoons aired Monday through Friday from 3:00 p.m. to 5:00 p.m., and then came the news and other programs. When my mom worked from 7:00 a.m. to 3:00 p.m., I would be so happy that she was around. When this wasn't the case, I knew she was working hard until late at night.

When she worked the 3:00 p.m. -11:00 p.m. shift, she had supper in the fridge with a note on the door. It usually read: *"The food is in the fridge. Warm it up and wash the dishes. Love, Ma."* She would cook before leaving for work. My dad had a serious look on his face when my mom wasn't around. I guess he also missed the boss of the kitchen. I would cherish the days when the family got together.

Many times, I found myself outside riding my bike and playing with my neighborhood friends. When it was family time (usually on Saturdays), my mother was the primary force to gather the family around the television. She usually didn't sit with us because she would be in the kitchen cooking or attending to other household chores. I could smell the *sofrito* as it sizzled in the pan, and as I walked into the kitchen I could see and hear the can opener as she opened a can of beans and the water running from the faucet as she drained and cleaned the rice. It was a different meal every day except Wednesdays, which was pasta night. The house filled with the delicious aromas of the *sofrito* ingredients my mother used to prepare our wonderful meals. Among the ingredients were garlic, onion, green peppers, recao, and aji peppers.

I didn't always know what to expect for supper, but I liked surprises and food was not excluded. At times, my mom surprised me with my favorite dish: good old homemade rice and beans with fried breaded shrimp. I would be in heaven, watching television and eating my favorite meal. I usually kept busy while she made dinner in the kitchen, staying out of her way as she cooked. The soft Spanish ballad music in the background kept her entertained in the kitchen.

I learned many songs by the Mexican singer, Jose Jose and the Spanish singers, Jose Luis Perales and Camilo Sesto. She would play their songs on the cassette player as she cooked everyday to the point that I knew every song in the order as they played.

My brother Luis and I had various household chores such as taking out the trash, cleaning our rooms, and washing the cars, which was fun because it provided an opportunity to play with the water hose. On Saturdays, the family gathered to talk to each other about school, things that were happening, and future plans. Television was a means for us to relate to one another without the outside pressures of everyday life. My mom enjoyed watching her *novelas*[20] on the Spanish channel during the weekday evenings and my dad usually read the newspaper. During the day, as she watched Jeopardy or Wheel of Fortune, I could hear her talking out loud as she answered questions given by the host. After my mom cooked supper on Saturday evenings, the family gathered around the television to watch a game show on the Spanish channel. When she tuned into *Sábabo Gigante*[21], I usually saw her with a big smile, laughing and cheering. I enjoyed seeing how the host made everyone laugh and feel united, both on television and at home.

I appreciated the joy exhibited by the people in the television studio, an audience comprised of happy, laughing people of all ages. The host man gave out prizes and money to people that participated and even cheered those that lost. The show was exciting and fun for all of us. It had competitions, famous singers and dancers were invited, and even new talented people appeared. There was a part where little kids were asked questions and they would respond with how they saw things from their own perspective, not from an adult point of view. The kids also showed their talents like singing and dancing. I stared at the television screen for three hours. The host would travel to different countries and interview people. I learned a lot about other cultures from his explanations of their customs and traditions. The show started in the evening and ended late at night, and I always fell asleep in front of the television. I would go to the bathroom only during commercial breaks. Also on commercial breaks, I could hear my mom washing the dishes and cleaning up the kitchen. Then, during commercial breaks later in the program, she would go into our rooms and prepare our beds for each of us. The family show was a television program not to be missed and never to be forgotten.

Ever since those days of my childhood and our family rituals, on Saturday evenings I still find myself making sure my chores and errands are done before the family show begins. Many years had passed when I saw an interview on television and learned that *Don Francisco* was his stage name. The man loved by so many of us had a different name, and that he and I shared the same first name. When I learned about it,

I was shocked. I could not believe the news I was hearing. His real name is Mario Luis Kreutzberger Blumenfeld, born in Chile and from German descent. I was surprised that the man who had made my mom so happy, whom everyone in the family had watched religiously every Saturday, had a personal connection with me. I was astonished when I learned about his real name. Not only had the television show made a difference in my house, but now I had a personal connection with the host. After many years, I came to learn that even my cousins, aunts, uncles, friends, and people in the Hispanic community shared the same joy when watching the Saturday evening family show. Today *Sábado Gigante* continues to be a part of my family's traditional Saturday ritual. Television has a powerful impact, not only on families but also on individuals and their way of connecting with the world. I thank Don Francisco for bringing my family together in a much-needed family spirit. To this day, I still see the family show *Sábado Gigante* aired on Univision, the Spanish-language channel aired across the United States and worldwide. When I call my family members on Saturday afternoon, they usually reply by saying, "I have to go watch *Sábado Gigante*." That brings a huge smile to my face, and sometimes I laugh because the tradition never changes, and the talented people on the show will amaze you. I encourage you to watch the show this Saturday and see for yourself.

"My best friends were like my family, and we all made up the street gang."

THE STREET GANG

During my high school Spanish class, I was introduced to many authors from Latin America and Hispanics from abroad. My Spanish teacher, Mrs. Rodriguez, made the class interesting and exciting. After assigning projects to the students, they had to give a show and tell in front of the class. Prior to attending her class, I had never enjoyed reading. I would see thick old books on the classroom shelves and the last thing on my mind was to pick one up. My Spanish teacher gave us a long list with the books that we were going to read in class, complete with deadlines. She described why we needed to read these books, told us when each test would be given, and on what material. Her idea was awesome, especially for an organized kid like me.

I remember the day that I met her. It was actually the year before she became my teacher. She asked me my name, and when I responded with Mario, she paused and then said she had some deep memories of a so-called Mario. She almost married a man named Mario. The teacher mentioned she had lived in New York City for some time, but being away from her family was unbearable. She missed her family and decided to move back to her hometown.

Mrs. Rodriguez was a great teacher and made her classroom inviting, but she was strict when it came with turning in our work on time. No one dared to cross her or disrupt the class. I was actually happy that no one did, because when the class was quiet I could hear everything she said and I could understand the material. One of the books on her list was *El Ingenioso Hidalgo Don Quijote de la Mancha* written by the Spanish author Miguel de Cervantes Saavedra. She had given us one hundred questions about the book, and without reading it, one could not know the answers.

Because I had to read so much and do my homework from other classes, I barely had time to have fun with my friends. They picked on me for being a nerd, an obedient student who really cared for school. Unlike me, they were fun, cool, and hated school.

During my high school years, my friends and I would walk to the countryside to explore. We went to people's farms and would get chased by watchdogs. That's when we ran home scared that the owners would catch us. On one particular visit to the country, we approached a hill that had a tall windmill. The windmill was huge and I felt so tiny. When I looked up and saw the windmill, it took me back to the time when I read the book my teacher had assigned. According to what I read, Don Quixote thought that windmills were huge ferocious giants trying to attack him. On this occasion, I believed that the windmill was a giant and that I was a tiny Smurf.

Although my friends attended school every day, some of them did not like it, but that did not deter me from being their friend. I was a bookworm and my friends gave me something I lacked: confidence. I was actually respected for being the way I was. I applied myself more and more at school and I grew to enjoy reading. As a result, I missed out on a lot of fun with my friends. I went to summer school just to take the next year's classes. I did this for two years and finished high school before my graduating class. For me, hanging out in front of our house and doing nothing was not productive. I was called *estofon*[22] by a lot by my friends. Fun was the name of my game. If I was going to leave my homework for later that night, I had to be doing something fun.

My brother was an amateur disc jockey and spent all his savings on compact discs, speakers, turntables and lighting. I thought he was crazy for spending so much money on expensive music equipment. Music had been sold in so many forms before, LPs to eight tracks to cassettes, and now it was CDs. I guess my brother had to buy all the latest music because he was the disc jockey for the neighborhood parties. It was his job to keep up with the latest music and party trends. Everyone expected that mirror ball spinning on the ceiling. It reflected rotating light onto the walls, just like in the good old disco fever times.

My brother's friends helped him set up parties around town. Our street gang was like a big family and similar to *The Little Rascals*[23]. Each of us had a different personality, yet all of us respected each other for being unique. We were each other's support system when we got punished by our parents. My friends were Chelo and Javier, neighbors from the next street. Xiomara was our front neighbor. Javier, Yajaira, and Sheila were brother and sisters; they lived next to us. Banchi and Ivanisse, also brother and sister, lived across the street. My cousin Chas, who I loved like a sister, my brother Luis and his girlfriend, Beba and her sister, Gary, and I made up the thirteen members of our group. This was our crazy street gang. We loved and hated each other at times.

With Chas being like our sister, we were overprotective of her from the boys at school. One time, around 9:00 p.m., she was with Ivanisse across the street. The gates of our house were locked. She called for someone to open them, but no one heard her, so she crawled between the gates at the top opening. She was so skinny that she could fit through any crack. On this occasion, when she pulled the gates enough to fit through, she put her feet in first and her face came through last. Somehow, the braces on her teeth caught on the rails and she began screaming for help. I heard all the screaming and didn't know what was happening, so I ran out to see what was going on. I saw her sort of hanging from the gate and grabbing it tightly. She slowly figured out a way to disconnect her metal braces from the gate and got down. She was scared and in a little pain, but then we laughed. A wire was hanging out of her mouth, so I then looked for some nail clippers and cut the piece off. From that day on, we told her to be in the house early and not to sneak in like she had tried to. Several months later she moved back to her parents' home in New York. I will never forget that moment and I know she won't either.

Banchi and Ivanisse's parents had a family van that my brother sometimes used to transport his music equipment. Awhile later, my parents got him an old white van, which he was always fixing because it was constantly breaking down. Ivanisse was several years younger than most of the gang, but she acted like an adult. Banchi had everything he wanted. They had a jet ski, expensive toys, a Chow Chow dog, numerous cars, and a sense of humor to go with it all. Their dog's named was Charlene. She was the house guardian with a lion-like appearance and if she didn't know you she would make her presence known. Banchi would brag that Charlene had a purple tongue and looked like a bear. I never contradicted him because it was all true.

Our neighbors next door were simple, humble and great people. Our neighbor's mom, Luz, was an excellent cook who specialized in pastries. She created giant cakes for parties and special celebrations. She worked at a local bakery. One time, we heard a large explosion that shook the ground. Everyone in the neighborhood ran outside to see what had happened. Our neighbor came out running, screaming, with her eyes wide and her hair pulled back. She was walking around with smoke all over her, but nothing was burning. Everyone ran to her rescue, but luckily she was not hurt and only several strands of her hair were burned. She told us that she had left the gas on high while she went in search of a match. When she returned minutes later and lit the match, the stove blew up. That was the loud explosion. Ever since that day, I have never played with matches or liked gas stoves. We had an electric stove at home, so that made me feel safe. That was a learning moment I would never forget.

My first kite competition was with my neighbor's father, Kako. He taught me how to make a giant kite with paper, glue, and small sticks. The kite festival was approaching, and it was a tradition for the people in town to plan ahead and create the biggest and most creative kites that actually could fly. Javier approached me one day and asked if I wanted to go to the kite festival. He said that we were all going to make kites and fly them there. I liked the idea, and joined him and his father. There I was, assembling pieces of plastic bags, glue, and sticks to make a kite. My kite came to be about five feet tall and three feet wide. Javier's father was patient and made a small and interesting paper kite. The rice paper his father used for the kite, a delicate, thin paper found in several colors, was expensive, so we decided to make ours with plastic bags. There was a box full of large bags under the kitchen sink. Two days later, on a hot Sunday morning, it was time to go to the kite festival, held in our town's baseball field. When we got there, the sky was full of homemade kites in a variety of designs and colors. Javier's father told me that the trick to maintaining the kite in the air was the balance of the weight of the kite itself and the weight of the tail. If the kite went from side to side, then more weight needed to be put on the tail. If it didn't fly high, then the tail was too heavy. This was where I learned to attach small bows at the end of the tail. I had always believed those small knots were for decorative purposes, but I was wrong. They were actually for balancing the entire kite to keep it from falling. That day, no one I knew won the kite competition. The prizes varied from the best-looking to the biggest and most creative. I really enjoyed my day in the park; it was cool seeing all the kites that filled the sky with a variety of interesting shapes and colors. I didn't go to win necessarily, but to have fun and experience something new, and someone curious like me could not miss out.

One of our neighbors from the next street was like a brother to us. Javier went to our school and was in the same classes as my brother. Javier taught me to drive a standard shift car in his brother's black Toyota Celica. He tried his best, but I needed to train my senses. I needed to look forward and move the shift with my right hand while my left hand was on the steering wheel. Then my left foot needed to be on the clutch, and my right foot needed to be on the gas pedal or brake. It was confusing at the time and scary when we were going uphill. If one does not know how to control a stick car on a hill, it may roll back momentarily when shifting into first. I gave up for several weeks until I felt the courage to try again. I must mention that the black Celica may have been cursed. I tried to learn to drive a stick shift, but never completely learned the craft in that car. The car moved abruptly, and I feared driving up hills because it would roll back down if I didn't give it gas and shift gears at the same time. On one occasion, after several attempts I gave up for the day and we switched seats. I moved from the driver's seat to the passenger's seat and Javier drove me home. When he dropped me off, I got out, and as I closed the door I accidentally slammed my index finger between the door and the car. I did not scream, but I started jumping up and down and ran inside to see my bruised index finger. My entire left hand and arm hurt as if someone had hit me with a baseball bat. For three months the skin under my nail was black. To this day, my nail does not grow normally and fully. In my understanding, either the car was cursed or that was my punishment for giving up my driving lesson.

One day, Javier and my brother Luis came home with bruises and scratches on their arms and faces. I thought they'd gotten into a fight, but both were laughing and joking around. I was a little confused with what was going on. Javier told me that they had been going to work in his car and had encountered an animal. He mentioned having the sunroof open. I really enjoyed when the sunroof was open all the way. You could get more air, see the sky, and stretch your arms. I was not prepared to hear what he said next. To my surprise, he was actually laughing and happy as he described what had happened.

Javier said that as he was driving the two of them to work, and as they approached the bridge that went over the lake, something unusual happened. The windows were open, and the radio was playing. Suddenly, it felt as if an animal wanted to attack them and take over the vehicle. They said at first they'd thought it was a chicken that wanted a ride to town, but actually it was a pigeon that had entered through the sunroof. It came in so fast and unexpectedly that Javier lost control of the car, sped to the side, and crashed head-on into the bridge side rails. Javier and Luis almost found themselves floating in the lake. Luckily, Javier's maneuvering skills were quick and the bird was not out to attack anyone. It just wanted a ride and boarded at the wrong place. I will always remember what happened that day because of the bruises and scratches they both had, along with the damage to the car.

On one of those crazy teenage days, our friends came up with the idea to make a *marquesina*[2] party, which is nothing more than a good old Puerto Rican style garage party. It was done by many people in the community. The idea was to have a good time with everyone we knew, especially our best friends. My brother was the DJ, and the gang and I were the fun go-getters. We all made it happen as a team. We set it up for a Friday, when everyone was able to stay up a little later and enjoy each other's company. Because my brother knew the ins and outs of a party, he set up a time to pick up some chairs from the local funeral home with his van. Yes, believe it or not, the local funeral home rented chairs. My buddies and I went around the neighborhood with a machete to find some palm tree branches. During our journey around the entire neighborhood, we asked the homeowners with palm trees if we could cut off some of the lower hanging fronds. We came home with scratches and bruises from climbing all those tall palm trees. Here and there, we found some palm fronds lying on the ground, but not enough for our purposes. Back home, we put the palm fronds on the metal rails that closed in the *marquesina,* which gave some privacy from the street and made it an intriguing tropical sight from afar.

Parties meant lots of music, potato chips, and soda. For us, that would constitute a party scene, along with all the neighbors and friends. There was always the disco mirror ball on the ceiling, a lot of eighties music, and lots of fun on the dance floor. My mom would be in her room watching *novelas* but sometimes came out to see how things were running.

Sometimes we would charge a fee at the entrance so that my brother could pay for his new music and DJ equipment. Overall, the *marquesina* parties were something I would never forget. Our friends in the neighborhood would take turns throwing parties and compete to see which party was the best. My best friends were like my family and we all made up the street gang in the *urbanización*[24] Vista Monte neighborhood in Cidra, Puerto Rico.

"She taught me a lesson about not giving up
on what I wanted no matter how simple it might be."

MI PUEBLO

Vote for blue, vote for red, vote for green—just VOTE! On a hot summer day, people gathered at the plaza de Cidra to yell and shout. People shouted and raised their flags as the man running for mayor gave several speeches to the public. He was from the *Partido Nuevo Progresista de Puerto Rico*—New Progressive Party of Puerto Rico. This particular party advocates for Puerto Rico statehood. They are the ones that want Puerto Rico to become the 51st State of the United States. The man spoke to the crowd about different things he was going to do if elected. He mentioned modernizing the city and renovating different public facilities. Just before he got in front of the crowd, many cars and trucks drove around the town honking their horns. The convoy of vehicles sported flags and had words written on the windows. There were several convoys every other week from different political parties. On one day, the cars would be decorated in blue with palm fronds representing the New Progressive Party, and then the next convoy would feature cars covered with red flags with a straw hat printed on them. The red flags represented the *Partido Popular Democrático* – Popular Democratic Party. Many people would shout "*Que viva la pava!*" (Long live the *pava*[25]). On another day, the people would have on green shirts and the cars would be decorated in green with a white cross. Those people would holler "*Queremos independencia!*" (We want independence). They represented the *Partido Independentista Puertorriqueño* – The

Puerto Rican Independence Party. Advocates of this political party campaign for the independence of Puerto Rico from the United States. They are usually called *pipiolos* and can be identified with the color green.

All of the convoys evoked a feeling of excitement and fun. I recall running to where all the noise was coming from. It didn't matter what colors were on the cars, I still shouted with joy for them. I would see other people do it, so I imitated their behavior. The feeling was contagious and fun at the same time. When one convoy passed by, several people might come out of their homes to cheer, and when another convoy passed by, out came the occupants of other houses.

Usually you would see older people, but young folks would still be cheering with every car that passed by. At times, the same people had all three colors. My family was conservative when it came to politics, so I never saw them cheering or standing at the corner yelling and having a good time like I was. My grandmother would tell me that dealing with politics could be dangerous because people became enemies if one didn't side with them. I never understood what she meant; I was just in my own little world and enjoying myself. I was not going to stop having fun because I knew I was not old enough to vote anyway.

Every time I heard loud noises coming from afar, I would run outside to see what was going on. Many months before Election Day, several people would tie a speaker to the roofs of their cars and announce the next political party candidate. It was accompanied by music and a theme song. Each political party had its own song, so when I heard the song, I could easily identify which party was approaching. My great-grandfather from my father's side, *Abuelo*[26] Toño would stay on the balcony and look at the cars passing by. When they were gone, he would still be there, staring away, leaning against the railings. He did that every day. Although he sided with the red color, (Popular Democratic Party) my other family members sided with the blue (New Progressive Party). The only people I knew who sided with the green (Puerto Rican Independence Party) were several of my teachers. They never told me directly, but I knew due to the color they displayed and their extreme patriotism behavior.

I learned a lot from my great-grandfather. *Abuelo* Toño was my grandmother's father on my father's side of the family. He was tall, thin, and very white. He was picky about what he ate. My grandmother would serve him breakfast every morning. One day he would eat only two hard-boiled eggs, crackers, and coffee. The next day she would serve him *maizena*,[27] crackers, and coffee.

He always walked upright in a straight position and used a brown cane. Not like what I used to see in other older folks at later stages of their elderly years, such as, having bent spines and difficulty walking. When he saw me, he often gave me a nickel. He was not too generous when it came to giving money away. Mentally he was still living in beginning of the 1900's. He taught me a lot about history and especially about our culture. He would talk very low, so I had to pay close attention in order to hear what he had to say. On one occasion, he sat me down and spoke to me the entire day. He was my teacher and I was his faithful student.

One time I asked him about the numerous black and white photographs hanging on his wall, all of which seemed to be of the same person. He told me the man was a famous person and well loved by many people. The man was a journalist, poet, and politician, and the first elected governor of Puerto Rico. He was in power for sixteen years and was part of the Popular Democratic Party. His name was Luis Muñoz Marín. He was the first democratically elected governor of Puerto Rico and referred as the "father of modern Puerto Rico."

"That is similar to the name of my school," I said.

Abuelo Toño told me that my school was named after this person's father, Luis Muñoz Rivera. I was amazed by this story and wanted to hear more and more. But my great-grandfather said he needed to go to work. He worked in a small wooden shack behind the house where he made cigars with his bare hands. Some days, I really didn't want to go play. I just wanted to observe him. He would sprinkle wine on the large leaves of tobacco before they dried up, and then he would place them on the empty bed in the front room of the house. In the shack, I sat down beside him and looked at his hands. He would take each tobacco leaf from the drying shelf, place the leaf on his small working table, and spread it out. He would dip his hand into a small container of water and sprinkle water onto the leaf to flatten it out. He then took shredded tobacco from a brown bag and placed it in the middle of the leaf. He took his sweet time and was very careful. He would then roll the tobacco leaf until it was completely rolled up. After cutting the edges and fitting it to the same size as the others, he would place it on the top shelf with the others. He had markings on the walls with worn notes on old paper. I saw the pile of cigars lined up. He sold the cigars to local people and gave them as gifts to his friends.

As he made his cigars, he would speak to me in a low voice, so I had to be very close to him and listen carefully.

He told me that the people of our *raza*[28] came from a mix of cultures. Now, this was something interesting I had to hear. He said that Puerto Ricans were a mix of three cultures: the Taino Indians, Africans, and Spaniards. I really did not understand what he was saying, but I asked him if that was why Puerto Ricans had different skin tones.

"Yes!" he responded in a louder voice.

As he spoke to me about many other things, customers came to the shack and called his name. People would come through the *callejón*[29] from the side of the house to buy the cigars. My mom told me that her father had bought cigars from him when they were both younger. *Abuelo* Toño sold his cigars for five cents when they were sealed in a box and ten cents for the loose ones.

When an elderly person was talking to you, it was disrespectful to leave without permission. But my great-grandfather would talk for hours, and sometimes his excessive stories about history bored me. Once he told me that he would go to the capital city on a horse to see the doctor and come home several days later. He said that in his youth, there was no television, electricity, or telephones, and that a man would come with a ladder to light the street lanterns. I was so intrigued with his stories that I considered them my history books.

I remember his 100th birthday, which we celebrated at the local Rotary club out in the country side, with my uncles, aunts, and cousins, along with neighbors and many family friends. It was a huge celebration that continued all afternoon until late at night. That was the first time I had ever seen all of my family members together. Several years later, my great-grandfather fell and hurt himself. The fall contributed to his weakness and he was confined to bed for some time and eventually passed away. He died at 107 years old.

I used to climb the guava tree next to the shack, to see the town from high above and to pick the guavas and give them to my grandmother. There was also a coffee tree, and I would pick the coffee beans from it and shoot objects with my slingshot. I always enjoyed being in the backyard. There was a washing machine that did not have a lid on it, with two rollers on the side which were used to wring the clothes. It was an old-fashion washer machine. I would see my grandmother go to the large cement *pileta*[30] and wash some clothes by hand using a blue bar of soap. She boiled starch on the stove and dip my grandfather's *guayaberas*[31] in it. Once she ironed them they were stiff and crisp. She would put all other clothes on the clothesline by the side of the house. When they were dry, she would take them off the line, fold them, and put them away.

Every Sunday, I would wake up early in the morning to a loud noise coming from the street. It was a small car with a loudspeaker on top of it. I would hear *"Hay pan"* (there is bread). People rushed out of their homes to the car and buy warm bread from the man. My grandma would also rush out and get some bread—*Pan Sobao' or Pan de Agua*,- run back to the kitchen table to cut it up and butter it, and serve it with breakfast.

During the summers we would also hear loud noises coming from the loudspeakers on advertising cars, announcing the *Fiestas Patronales*[32] were coming to town soon. The festivities were celebrated in the center of town, around the church located in the middle of the plaza. Community members would decorate the plaza and a carnival would come for an entire week. There would be cotton candy, a merry-go-round, and other amusement rides. One could barely walk due to the large crowd. The town was so small that I would see many of my family, friends, and classmates there. All four streets surrounding the main plaza area were full of people and carnival rides. There was a small theater in front of the church, and one day while we were waiting for the ticket men to arrive, my father took me into the theater to see *The Smurfs*[33]. That was the first movie I had ever seen on the big screen. I'll never forget the first day of the festival. Everyone in my family wanted to be there. Many people would gather and walk around the street with a huge statue of our patron saint, *Nuestra Señora del Carmen*.[34]. She was carried on an altar-like platform with people holding it up high. People would pray and have flowers in their hands. At night there were fireworks, and the people of the town were the happiest folks around.

One day after school, I asked my father if I could go to my classmate's house and he said no. I knew he was very strict and overprotective, and letting us out of his sight was a no go. I wanted to go out because I was a bored that day. My grandmother asked me to go to the house of her sister, who we called *Titi*[35] Toñin, to get some eggs. This was about half a mile away up the hill. Her sister had chickens all over the backyard and they ran in and out of the house as well. When I got there I was so excited to see them. The chickens and roosters were all over the place-on the table, windowsills, and even under the table. She wore bifocal glasses so maybe she could not see them all over the house. The doors were wide open, which allowed them to come and go as they pleased. There was a hen with about eight little chicks following her everywhere.

I told my great-aunt that I had been sent by my Grandma Luisa to get some eggs. She went outside to get some from a nest. In the meantime, I was staring at the hen and chicks. She came back several minutes later with a basket full of large brown eggs, which she rinsed off in the kitchen sink. While she was drying them and putting them in a brown bag, I asked if I could have a small chick to take home as a pet. She told me that the hen would be upset if I took a little one away, but she said she could give me a young chicken that was a little older than the baby chicks. I was so happy when she told me that. "Follow me," she said, leading me toward the yard. Little did I know what was going to happen next. "Are you ready to run?" I heard her say.

I looked at her and asked why.

"Before I can give you a chicken, you must catch it," she said, pointing toward the bird she had in mind.

I started running, and the only thing I heard was the poor chickens making strange noises. I got close to several other hens with chicks and the hens chased me away. Then a rooster came after me. I was running around in circles trying to catch the small chicken while the big rooster chased me. I was laughing so much that I found myself giving up. Titi Toñin told me that unless I caught the chicken, I could not take it home. I told her that I had given up chasing the poor chicken, and that I would return home with only the eggs I had come for.

"Don't give up so easily," she said, looking at me. "Giving up is a habit that will be hard to break when you grow up."

After I reflected on what she'd said, she told me to follow her. In the backyard shack, she guided me toward a bucket of corn. There were several empty containers of different sizes and colors on the ground. "Take a container and fill it with corn," she said. Then she took me to the tool section and told me to grab the long pole with a net at the end. Outside, she told me that I should never give up, no matter what. She was going to teach me how to catch a chicken her style. She told me to place the corn on the ground only when the net was next to the area where the chickens were going to eat. She took the corn away from me while I placed the net around the area she told me to. In a pleasant tone of voice, she called, "Are you ready?"

"Ready for what?" I asked.
"To catch your first chicken."

"I think so."

"You don't need to run this time," she said.
I was a little confused, but I knew she had more experience than I did.

"Go to the end of the pole attached to the net and watch what happens next," she said, and as soon as she scattered the corn on the ground, all the chickens and roosters ran to the corn. They were all hungry and ready for their meal. When the small chickens arrived, I waited for the white chicken I wanted to take home, but it never showed up. We waited for a while, and then she told me to flip the net. We gathered around the net and she placed a towel over it. She lifted the net and grabbed a small gray chicken. "You can take this one home," she said.

We went inside and she put the chicken into a large brown paper bag. She told me to wash my hands and to be careful not to drop the eggs I was also taking. As I was leaving, I said, "I really wanted the white chicken I'd seen earlier in the yard."

"You never get what you want when you give up, but you might get something close to it." I soon realized that had I not given up, I would have been taking home the chicken I really wanted. She taught me a lesson about not giving up on what I wanted, no matter how simple it might be. I would have to persist with courage until my goal was met. I gave her a kiss and said *"Bendición,"* and she replied with, *"Dios te bendiga, mijo.*[36]*"*

While I was walking on the sidewalk going down the hill approaching my grandmother's house, I saw everyone cheering and yelling. It was because of a convoy of cars with blue flags with palm trees on them. The music was joyful and happy. I remembered the song from past months. They were the people from the plaza that past summer. I recognized the man's voice on the loudspeaker recording. The man who had persisted in making a big difference in our town had won the election. People called him "Wiso". Angel L. Malave Zayas became the Mayor of Cidra in November of 1989, representing the New Progressive Party. As the months passed, many things changed in town. All the streets were repaved, new trees were planted, and the streets were much cleaner. I guess the new mayor did make a great difference. No one had to tell me because I saw the positive changes for myself.

One morning around five thirty, I woke up due to the loud music in the distance. It was far away, but I heard it getting closer and closer. It got so loud that I opened the front door and saw many other people on their balconies as well. My grandmother also came to the balcony. To my surprise, it was the mayor and a group of people singing and playing instruments. They were all on the back of a white truck giving a *serenata.*[37] The mayor was throwing carnations to the older women standing on the sidewalk and on the balconies, many of them with tears of joy in their eyes. My Grandma Luisa told me that it was Mother's Day and the mayor was honoring the mothers in our town. That spring morning will eternally live in my heart. My grandma had a big smile on her face and became sentimental by hearing the music.

The town of Cidra is known as *La Ciudad de la Eterna Primavera*.[38] In this town, I attended Luis Muñoz Rivera Elementary School, Jesús T. Piñero Middle School, and Ana J. Candelas High School. All were located near the center of town. The baseball team was known as *Los Bravos*[39] of Cidra. In previous years they had been the National Championship Team of Puerto Rico. They were famous in town, but I never got to meet any players. The only baseball player I knew by name was the legendary Latino Roberto Clemente, who was from Carolina, Puerto Rico. I learned in school that he had played for the Pittsburgh Pirates in the United States from 1955 until his death on December 31, 1972. Clemente died in a plane crash en route to Nicaragua, where he planned to deliver emergency supplies to earthquake victims. His mother, Doña Luisa, shared the same name as my grandmother.

Although I moved to the United States after graduating high school, I will always be a true *jíbaro*[40] and *Cidreño*[41] in my heart, no matter where I am in this world. I will never forget the many times I went to the Cidra lake, the Sabanera Pigeon Festivals, or the Patron Saint Festivals, or the hours I spent attending Mass, swimming at the pond with my school friends, seeing the baseball games at the park, or having fun on Tomas Maestre Street, the road where both of my parents grew up, and I had the same pleasure of being part of the memories that took place on that special street. All of my memories will continue to be cherished in a special place with me and I will never forget *mi pueblo*.[42]

"I still ask myself what really matters –
having the pleasure to win, or having the pleasure to lose."

FIFTEEN MINUTES OF FAME

Competing with others has always been something I've kept on the back burner. I've never liked competing or trying to be better than others who share my same craft. My high school art teacher had faith in me. He believed I had a talent and urged me to pursue my passion for art. In high school I was a quiet student and never looked for trouble. I recall that I had approached the middle school art teacher because I was interested in taking the art class, but could not sign up because his classes were full. It made me sad that something I really enjoyed doing was unavailable to me at school. So I continued making art on my own until I reached high school, where art was also an elective. I approached the art teacher, Mr. Muñiz, and told him that I was interested in taking his class. The period with available space was actually assigned to twelfth graders, and I was an eleventh grader, but he allowed me to register so long as I did the required work. I was surprised that all my friends noticed a change in me. They believed I had done something and was hiding it from them. I was always serious, and displaying my happiness was a rare thing.

The first day of class, the art teacher gave us a list of art materials to purchase at the local art store. When I got home, I told my mom that I had gotten the class I wanted. She was happy for me, and gave me $20.00 to buy the materials I needed and for the class fee. I believe my enthusiasm for the art class raised my academic achievement in my other classes. I did not do to well during my middle school years. I guess I felt more motivated in high school and more willing to participate because I was happy.

The art class was the last class period of the afternoon. Even after attending class all day, I entered my art class full of energy and enthusiasm. After the bell rang, I often remained in the classroom to finish my work, along with several teachers and students who also stayed late. Walking to the bus station, I had to cover my paintings and other projects because people would constantly stop me to see my artwork. They always complimented me, but also made my walk to the bus station seem much longer. I never considered myself a showoff and never liked the added attention.

The work I did in art class was open to my own creativity and imagination. After we did the required art projects, we could create anything we wanted as long as the materials were used wisely. I never misused the materials and never put any artwork in the trash. When I started a project, I made sure I was disciplined enough to complete it. The word got out in school that I was a good artist, but to me, I was a normal kid with a little artistic talent.

Because I was in the class of seniors, I became acquainted with many of them. The seniors took a trip to a televised game show called A Toda Maquina[43], which aired on Channel 6. The show consisted of two schools competing against each other in various academic and artistic categories. During the student selection, I was chosen, even though I was not a senior. I guess my reputation had helped me gain a ticket to hang out with the seniors. Usually, the students that competed in these competitions were smart and high honor students. I felt honored that my talent was on par with theirs. I was told the day before that I would be competing against a student from another school in the drawing category. I was thrilled and nervous at the same time. There I was, thinking about what I would do and what to say. I was never a good public speaker and didn't like pressure. It was only years later that I developed patience and the ability to tolerate stress and pressure when it came to art projects.

The morning of the trip arrived and I was nervous and anxious for the whole thing to be over with. Before I left to school that morning I was pacing back and forth in my bedroom thinking about what to draw and say. The teacher in charge called the roll, and there I was, the last student on the list. I was usually the last one to be called in the classroom because my last name started with a "V." At the bus, I felt out of place and alone. I didn't know everyone on the bus, only the students in my classroom. Twenty minutes later, a beautiful young girl with glasses and long hair approached me. I recognized her because she lived down the street from me. She never played outside, but I would see her on the bus that took us home. She talked to me and said some comforting words. She was as nervous as I was, and she had been the one who picked me to compete. She mentioned to me that someone had told her that I was a good artist. She explained that there was no senior artist and she had needed someone for that category. I felt humbled and proud that she had picked me, but that gave me even more anxiety because I was already expected to win even before I had competed. She told me that a winner's attitude would help me win and that positive thoughts would make things easier.

When the bus parked in front of the television station, my heart began to beat very fast. Everyone on the bus was a stranger to me and yet I over heard they expected me to win for them. They were encouraging, cheering each other and chanting songs along the hour bus ride to the television station. Many were practicing words, diction, studying for unexpected questions, and so forth. I noticed each of them wanted to win and take the trophy back to school. Inside the studio, it all became real to me. It was no longer a fantasy of thinking that being on television would be a thing of another world.

Each school was assigned an identifying color. The students participating stayed in the back, practicing what they were going to compete in. I was told to draw a dove. The *Sabanera* dove was a symbol of the town of Cidra in which our school was located. Two hours later, it was my turn to compete. I was taken to a desk that had markers and crayons on it, and a huge television camera was placed in front of me. When it was time for the drawing competition, the camera was placed even closer to me. I could see the red light was on in front of the square metal box. That meant it was recording everything I was doing. There was a man standing behind the camera to maneuver it. The game show host stood next to me and said that I had fifteen minutes to complete my drawing.

Those fifteen minutes felt like fifteen seconds. I was perspiring due to the heat of the lights and from being nervous. When the time was up, I lifted my drawing and got a little dizzy. I was so nervous that when the man with a microphone asked me to explain my drawing I was speechless. I could not say the correct words to explain my drawing. Under the bright lights, the camera was still aimed in my direction and the studio audience was looking straight at me. The studio was quiet. I said several words that made no sense. When the lights that were pointed at me were turned off, everything went away. The host, camera, and audience all were then focused on the other contestant. For me, his drawing was terrible, and I knew that it was not at competition level according my standards. But when he spoke, he described his drawing in a way that convinced the judges that it meant something. His drawing was somewhat abstract, it had circles and wild marks without any specific depiction of something identifiable, but his detailed explanation conveyed a sense of understanding and clarity.

So my drawing was much better, but my competitor expressed himself with true, deep feeling. I was impressed with his words, not with his art. I felt that I had let down my school and the people who believed in me. I left the studio feeling sad, and thinking a lot about what I could have said to express my feelings. I was told by the senior coordinator at school what to draw. I never felt I was going to lose. That day, I learned that drawing and explaining something that didn't come from the heart was not authentic. The pressure of everyone wanting me to win was actually my downfall. However, although I didn't win my category, my school earned enough points to win the overall competition.

While on my way to school the next day, I was stopped by a group of elementary school students. In order to get to the high school, I had to pass in front of the elementary school I had attended several years earlier. The children wanted my autograph because they had seen me on television. I was amazed and surprised by this. I said that I had lost the drawing competition and my autograph was worthless. One little girl said, "The important thing was that you tried." I laughed and smiled at all of them. After hearing that, I had a big smile on my face and gave my autograph. I guess even losing gave me my fifteen minutes of fame. Thanks to those little kids who stopped me on the sidewalk, I learned that the importance of a competition is not always winning, but trying and participating. I was never approached with critical remarks about my performance on the show and for losing that day. I was still a talented artist; I just didn't win that day. I still ask myself what really matters—having the pleasure to win, or having the pleasure to lose.

During the early spring, my art teacher approached me and said he wanted me to enter another competition, along with several of my classmates. He explained that the artwork had to convey a message of the folklore and customs of our youth. It was something broad yet interesting. I could come up with any idea as long as it conformed to the contest rules. He gave me the measurements of the board I needed to buy and a materials list for this specific project. After I made several sketches, he agreed that I should go with one of a boy playing a native guitar. After gathering all the materials, I was ready to start. I dedicated all my spare time to this project.

At first, it was not that important to me because I never enjoyed competing. But it did keep me busy and dedicated to my art. I hated trying to prove myself. It was a feeling of challenge and stress. I didn't create art to prove myself or my talent to anyone. I made art for my own pleasure and to express myself. I had created art since I was a little boy. If people liked it, that was fine; if they did not, that was fine with me, too.

Two weeks later, my teacher told me that the date for submission was approaching and I needed to finish what I had started. He could notice by my facial expressions that day that I was not motivated, and seeing the artwork of the other students, I was in for even more competition. The other students in the art room were great artists and some even more talented than I was. I began finalizing the drawing with the necessary details. Overall, it was a simple painting, but it had a powerful meaning. The youth were losing their interest in the native folklore traditions. It was rare to see a young boy playing a native guitar. Usually it was older and much more experienced grown men.

During the holidays, I used to see the *trovadores*,[44] who were singers of the typical native music of the island. There would be many older people singing such songs, but children rarely participated. Because of this, I sensed that my painting was conveying a strong message. I had no more explanation for my drawing. A fortunate aspect of this drawing competition was that I didn't have to explain my drawing to anyone.

The rules stated that I had to safeguard the edges and corners and surface of my work for shipping purposes, and I was required to use a media that would not smudge. The art teacher handled the shipping for me, so I didn't have to worry about it. The day had come when it was time to say goodbye to my artwork. It was the last time I would see the painting at school. The rules stated that the artwork would become the sole property of the contest committee. I never took a picture of it and didn't save my sketches. So the artwork had to live on its own, without any trace of me.

Months passed and I never heard any news about the artwork I submitted. The art teacher told me to forget about it and not to worry. I would have to get used to losing my artwork when I competed in art competitions. One day, the counselor came to the classroom door and told the teacher that he had an important phone call and needed to go to the office. She stayed with us until he returned. When he came back, he said that everyone who had submitted artwork in the art competition months earlier would be required to attend an open ceremony. I was nervous and asked him what the ceremony was for. He said the winners would be revealed, and that all participants were requested to attend.

I soon felt anxious and worried about how to get to the ceremony location. I knew my parents had busy schedules and might not have time to attend. The teacher said it would take place in a government building auditorium in the San Juan metropolitan area. Our high school was located an hour south of San Juan, and I knew travel would be a problem. When I got home that day, I told my parents the news and my mom agreed to take me. She worked at the Veterans Hospital at 1 Veterans Plaza in San Juan on the same route of the place we needed to be and was familiar with the area.

As the day approached, I needed to get new clothes for the occasion and take the day off from school. The ceremony took place on a school day and I was not comfortable missing class, but this was a rare thing. When the day came to report to the place I had written down, I was not as anxious as I had thought I would be. I guess having my mom with me eased the process and my nerves. My mom drove to the place, and finding parking was a hassle because there were so many cars, busses, and people. I had never attended an event like this.

This was the morning of May 6, 1993. The ceremony and the contest were sponsored by the government and the participants came from the entire island. There were many students and their parents from many high schools. The auditorium was packed, but there were still seats available when we arrived. It was hot due to so many people gathered in one location. There were no assigned seats, so we were on our own to find seats. I remember seeing a tall blonde woman who played a children's character on television. I saw several news crew people and their cameras. I noticed the government channel crew dominated the other private television crew members because it was a government-sponsored activity.

The walls were covered up to the ceiling with drawings and paintings. I guess they were the artworks of the participants. I remember my mom and I searching for mine. We couldn't see it. I said maybe there were too many to put them all up. I was a little disappointed, but still happy I could see who had won. The speakers on stage spoke about the importance of art and the process of creation. It was a touching and inspiring moment. All the speakers gave a synopsis of their experience and the impact of school on their talent.

On stage were three easels covered in white drapery, with spotlights illuminating them. My mom said the covered ones might be those of the students that had won. I didn't pay much attention because the speakers had interesting anecdotes I wanted to hear. A little more than half an hour had passed and it was time to uncover the paintings. When the person on the stage uncovered the first painting, the first winner was called up to receive his award. He went up, shook the hand of the female speaker, and stood beside several other important people for photographs. The second student was called, and she went up and did the same thing. The audience was clapping, cheering, and taking photographs. The audience was silent as the person stood beside the third painting, ready to reveal it. When the third cover was lifted, I saw my painting. The painting that I thought had been lost among the other paintings had indeed survived. I was shocked and excited. When the person went to the podium she called my name. She said, "The third winner is Mario Luis Vazquez." My eyes opened wide and I had a huge smile on my face. I walked to the podium, sweating and nervous. My mom stood up, began to cry, and was clapping. I was handed the award and stood there while many pictures were taken. The television cameras were all lined up at the bottom of the stage. The members of the audience were standing, clapping, and cheering. I felt so proud of myself and I felt humbled. I felt I no longer needed to prove myself, my talent, or my love for art. It had been acknowledged that I indeed had a talent for art, and was a winner at heart.

Minutes later when I was seated, many people came up to congratulate me. They were happy to see my artwork displayed on the stage. Even though I was the third place winner and not the first, I was one proud little boy at that moment. My mom started to cry again and I saw her tears of joy at my accomplishment. The theme of the contest was *"Fiesta Folklorica de la Juventud"* (Folklore Party of the Youth).

All three winners received monetary prizes as well. The first prize was one thousand dollars, the second prize was five hundred dollars, and the third prize was three hundred dollars. I was not expecting money as a prize. I was happy enough to be given the opportunity to participate and acknowledged. From that day on, my fellow classmates, teachers, and friends believed in me and I sensed their respected towards me. I was popular in school only for my talent. From then on, I felt awkward having so many people approach me. They wanted sketches made, ideas, and my story of how I had developed my artistic talent. I answered them that my talent was a gift I was born with, and that my schooling had not given me the talent but had perfected it. A week later I was watching television, and to my surprise, I saw my painting with several others being announced on the *Galleria de Telemundo*.[45] Telemundo was Channel 2 and broadcast its signal across the island. I was so happy to see my work on a television commercial. I knew I was not going to get it back, but I was so happy to know that it was going to be safe.

My middle school art teacher never gave me the opportunity to take his class. I never saw him again, and maybe I did not want to see him again. But I want to thank my high school art teacher, wherever he is, for giving me the opportunity to attend his class and for believing in me. I did so much better in my other classes due to his support. He was a quiet, passive, yet talented human being. I will never forget the opportunity I was given during my high school years, and, thanks to him, I had improved my craft. I encourage everyone to express themselves by any means possible, be it music, dance, sports, singing, acting, or any of the performing and visual arts. Expressing oneself and creating will change your life for the better, as it did mine. Try it and you will see for yourself that you will encounter a life-changing experience.

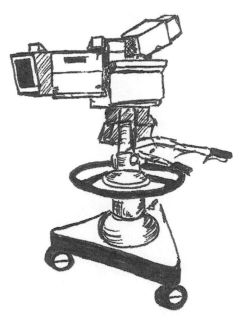

"My life up to that point had been so different,
and was like a book with many chapters of learning
experiences."

MY OWN DOG TAGS

It was the spring of 1994 when several men from the U.S. Army visited our high school to talk with the senior class. I didn't know what they were doing there, I just remember them looking like my uncle Garcia, who was also in the military. The men wore dark green pants, shiny black shoes, and light green crisply ironed shirts. Some of them had ribbons and things hanging from their sleeves, perhaps awards or merit ribbons. They entered a big classroom next to the main office of the high school. Signs were posted around the school with information about a military entrance exam. I had not signed up for the test, but sure was curious about it. The military had always interested me, and I was curious to see if they were hiring for jobs. I didn't know the requirements or academic standards needed, and I still had several months to go before graduation.

Years prior, I'd seen television programs and read newspaper stories about the Gulf War. Soldiers would greet their family members over the television in hopes that they would be watching on our side. The soldiers would mention their town and what military unit they were part of. I remember the economic difficulties the war caused among us. The price of food, utilities, and gas fluctuated a lot, worrying everyone in my family.

In middle school, a research project for my history class required my investigation of the specific causes and consequences of the war. All the middle school kids played outside like nothing was happening. The project was to be done on our own. The teacher just mentioned that America was at war and history was in the making. She never mentioned the reasons or her own opinions, so I can't say that I learned those directly from her. It was my job to read the newspapers and find out for myself. I needed a lot of visuals and explanations for the images I found. After reading the newspaper, I would cut out articles and save them until I had a large amount of information to process and write about. I got an A+ on my project. I figured the more images I had and the more writing I did, the better my grade would be. The report was so thick, like a huge scrapbook. The military people at the high school took me back in time, and reminded me about the war and what I had experienced by reading about it in the newspapers and watching the coverage on television.

Despite the Gulf War, I was still interested in someday being like my uncle Garcia. The men in uniform at school were Army National Guard recruiters. As I was walking down the hall, a recruiter invited me into the classroom where they had set up their information desk. One recruiter mentioned that he traveled a lot, lived in other countries, and had a secure income. Those words were convincing, but I was still undecided what my next step in life after high school would be. I was really interested in becoming a painter or some type of artist, but I still lacked the information on career paths.

Minutes later, the same recruiter approached me and asked if I wanted to take the entrance exam. I inquired about the requirements and benefits, and soon after our brief discussion, he signed me up to take the test.

A few weeks later I found myself seated at a desk in that same large room, with an answer sheet and booklet in one hand and a pencil in the other. I was taking the Armed Services Vocational Aptitude Battery (ASVAB). It was a multiple choice test that lasted for several hours. It was used to determine my qualification for enlistment into the United States armed forces. The recruiter told me that the options of my job choice would depend on my test results. I continued following the instructions from the booklet. The test lasted many hours and required too much thinking. At the end, I was exhausted and my brain was drained. When I finished, they told me to return to the same room in two weeks for the test results. It was already the end of the school day and I was dismissed to go home.

The two weeks passed and I was anxious to get my results. The recruiter had indicated that it was not a pass or fail test. Rather, a number in each category that indicated my potential competency in a specific field. I didn't understand that method, because in all my years of schooling, I had only known about A, B, C, D, or F grades, and the percentages allocated to the letter grades. It was odd, but I guess they knew what they were doing. When my name was called, I was told to make an appointment to talk about my options in job choices. I said I was still in high school and was not interested in leaving school to join the military. The recruiter replied that I could remain in school and work part-time only one weekend a month. That was indeed how the Army National Guard works. Many ideas came to mind about how I could use the money by working and going to school. For several days I thought about what the recruiter had said. I recalled all my family members who had served and still were serving in the military.

My mom's uncle, Tio Diego was a retired Sergeant First Class, my other cousin Javier was a lieutenant. My uncle Garcia was in communications. My cousin Leslie was in finance and her brother little Manny was in the Navy. My mom's brother, uncle Wallace served in the Vietnam War in 1969. My other cousin Angelo was also in the Army. I admired all of them for serving, but they lived so far away that none of them could give me advice in my difficult decision making process. I was telling myself that if they had done it, then I could do it. I was trying to convince myself that I would join the military and have a job.

At school, I asked my teachers what they would have done in my situation. Some were reserved with their answers, and others said that it would be a life changing experience. I didn't understand what the teachers meant; I just absorbed all of their advice. They pretty much stayed neutral and never gave me an indication to join or not join. I wonder why I never got a clear answer from the teachers; they had treated us like their own children while at school. I never gave it much thought; I just figured it out on my own.

My parents were not too supportive of the idea of me joining the military. My father was an only child, so he never would have been called for duty in the mandatory draft during his teenage years. My mom told me how she had considered joining the military as a nurse, but instead of enlisting; she worked as a civilian nurse at the Veterans Hospital. So, I was left to make a decision that would affect the rest of my life. I still thought about going to college, but was realistic about needing money to live on while in college. I knew I couldn't depend on my parents forever, and selling my art was not enough to survive. I realized that sooner or later I would have to grow up and experience life as an adult. My independence was the true reason that convinced me to consider the military and support myself throughout my college years.

After making my decision to finally join the military, I first told my mom. She was not at all content about my choice and it made her cry. She said that she would pay for school and I didn't have to join the military for the money reasons. That left me feeling guilty, as I would still be dependent on my parents. I was feeling that I could be less of a burden if I joined and started paying for my own expenses. The recruiter at school called my house and asked to make an appointment to talk to my parents and myself. We agreed that no decision was to take place the afternoon of the meeting and there was no guarantee that I would sign any papers forcing me to join.

Several days passed, my mom seemed sad, and I felt a sense of detachment. I wanted my independence and I wanted to go to college, and she still wanted to help me by paying my way through college. She always stressed the importance of education. She reminded us that the more schooling we had under our belts, the better our chances of getting a job that paid well. I was still undecided about what I wanted to study in college. I knew I was talented in art, but did not know if selling my artwork would be sufficient to help me survive.

I wanted to be a pilot, and even got a pilot symbol put on my senior class ring. When I told my grandmother the news of wanting to fly airplanes, it broke her heart. She told me that it was too dangerous and that she preferred that I not pursue that type of career. I respected and loved my Grandmother Luisa so much that I didn't think about it again. My class ring would always remind me of that dream of flying a plane someday, but due to my grandmother's wishes, it would remain a dream in her honor.

I also liked geography, psychology, and architecture. Still, I was undecided as to what career I would pursue in the long run. I remember looking at the letter carrier delivering mail around our neighborhood. I told my mom that one day I would like to be a mailman. Once, when the letter carrier approached our house with letters in hand, I asked her what the requirements to become a letter carrier were. She said I had to take a test and when an opening was available I would be called. Because the town we lived in was so small, the chances of me getting a postal job were slim. I would have to wait for someone to retire or transfer out of town. Those two reasons made it nearly impossible, and many other people were on the waiting list hoping to be called. So the possibility of joining the military was becoming clear in my mind.

One day the phone rang, and it was the recruiter again, announcing that he would be at my home within an hour. I was nervous during the time waiting for him. I didn't want to show my mom that I was nervous because she might have canceled the appointment. When the recruiter approached the house in a white car with a license plate that read U.S. Government, I sensed that I was going to be in that car one day soon.

It was February 1994, and I had several months to go in high school, so that relaxed my mom. It was her day off, so when the recruiter came in the house, my mom greeted the man and gave him a glass of water. He sat at the dinner table with his briefcase and pulled out a pack of papers. He said that he would go over my options, and that nothing would be guaranteed on exactly what career I would be chosen for. He said that because I wanted to go to college and was interested in the military, he would sign me up for the Army National Guard.

The recruiter explained that the Army National Guard had a college payment program that helped pay for full-time college students, and the Montgomery GI Bill would help with other expenses acquired while in college. I looked at my mom and thought that would be the answer to my prayers. I could still go to college and not depend on my parents for financial support. She was not too happy about the situation. I could see how serious she was during the entire time she was having a conversation with the recruiter. It seemed that my mom would be losing me, and I would be the sole property of the United States government. I recall my cousins and uncles in the military would be gone for months and even years at a time. We barely saw them.

It was a stresseful moment. Soon after I signed on the dotted line, the recruiter gave us copies of what I had signed, shook my hand, and said he would come back to pick me up after I graduated high school. He also gave me an address of the unit I would report to so I could get acquainted with the location and the people I would be working with after I returned from basic training. I couldn't believe how fast it all hit me. That spring was the fastest and most confusing time of my life. I didn't know what would happen to me next. In the summer of 1994 I graduated from Ana J. Candelas High School in Cidra, Puerto Rico.

When summer ended, the recruiter came back to my house in his white car, ready to pick me up. He said I just needed a backpack with several white shirts, jeans, and basic hygiene items. He said I was going to a mini basic training and not to worry too much. I didn't know there was such a place. Days prior I said goodbye to my friends in the neighborhood and my family, so when the recruiter arrived it was not too emotional. He took me to a military camp located in the south central part of the island. He said not to worry because my family and friends could visit me during visitation times on the weekends.

Then I was taken to a military camp located deep in a valley of the island, where I was given military uniforms, black combat boots, brown towels, brown underwear, and even brown handkerchiefs. They cut everyone's hair down to nothing; every recruit looked the same. It was all becoming a fast reality. At age seventeen, I was a soldier and was now called Private Vazquez. No one called anyone by his or her first name.

I realized that it was no longer a thought in my mind. It was a reality. I was now a member of the United States military. I spent several weeks there and learned basic military customs such as marching, exercises, and survival skills. The military camp concentrated not only on teaching the military way of life, but on perfecting our grasp of the English language. Since the citizens of Puerto Rico do not speak English in their everyday lives, new recruits were sent to a school to develop and practice their English language skills.

We were not allowed to speak Spanish and were forced to communicate in English. That was the only way students would learn, by being forced to speak English. Soldiers caught speaking the native language of the island would be punished. That meant long hours of doing guard duty, cleaning bathrooms, KP duty (kitchen police), and doing pushups. I found myself for hours shining my combat boots at night until a spit shine appeared. During morning inspections the drill sergeants could tell which soldier was dedicated due to their appearance. That included an unwrinkled ironed uniform, shinny boots and clean-shaven. During the late night hours while the soldiers were off duty the drill sergeants would sneak behind the doors to hear if the soldiers were speaking Spanish. On one occasion while the lights were out one sergeant was standing near the door and heard an entire conversation in Spanish by two soldiers. He blew a whistle and said everyone out of the building. We were on the second floor so he made us march downstairs in our underwear and make a line. He made us do push ups for about 30 minutes. He mentioned the Private talking in Spanish and he wanted to remind everyone that because we were in the military we needed to act like a team at all times. That meant if one person made a mistake it affected everyone in the Battalion. All the soldiers were sweating and very upset. I could hear several soldiers moaning and making noises of pain. I couldn't believe that at 10:45 at night I was already sleeping and because of another person not following the rules I was also punished. This taught me a lesson about team work and to be careful of my future actions.

On September 2, 1994, I was a graduate of the Puerto Rico Army National Guard Military School System located in Juana Diaz, Puerto Rico. Recruits could not leave or graduate without passing their English comprehension exam with a high score. I was relieved to have graduated because it was late summer and the weather was hot and humid.

After graduation, I spent my last days with my family. Soon, the recruiter returned to my house for his final trip. I was sent with my recruiter and a memorandum to the San Juan Military Entrance Processing Station at Fort Buchanan for the final stages of my civilian life. It was early in the morning when all the recruits were lined up and fully inspected for any marks, diseases, or disabilities. Our processing took about twelve hours. From blood tests to walking like ducks semi-nude was all part of the physical examination. Just before 8 p.m. that evening, half of the recruits that started the day were sent to a small room. We were told that we twelve were the only ones of the twenty-four recruits to have passed the physical. It was interesting to know that only half of so many were in the proper physical condition to join the military. People with eye problems, weight, and physical limitations were all disqualified. I guess I was a healthy young man. My mom's rice and beans and good Spanish cooking had paid off after all.

In the room I saw military flags and emblems along with a fancy red rug. I suppose it was an important room. The person in front of the recruits was a captain in uniform. He said to raise our right hands and repeat the words after him. After saying everything, he congratulated us for being part of the largest employer in the nation, and said that serving the United Stated military was an honor and a privilege, and that the experiences we would soon have would be lifelong lessons. He then said to preserve and respect the rights of all citizens, and to honor our past and fallen heroes.

The next morning, I had military orders to report to Fort Sill, Oklahoma, where I would remain for the next four months. There I became a 13E – Fire Cannon Direction Specialist in the Field Artillery branch. I was a transformed human being and would see the world from a different perspective. To this day, I've never been the same person. I was transformed from an adolescent into a strong-willed, disciplined soldier. It was a lonely path. I was away from my family, friends, and the people I loved the most. I became a proud soldier and truly experienced in training what I had read about in the newspaper war articles many years before. I was part of a team that would defend and honor the civil rights of all people, both at home and abroad. In the news I heard that the United States was seen as the leading military force in the world, and as such, bore a responsibility to help defend all people.

After basic training and my time in Fort Sill, Oklahoma, I returned to my National Guard Unit to attend college. I then moved to Connecticut where my family had moved. The job that I once had desired in my confusing teenage years became a reality: I was hired as a postal worker in Stratford, Connecticut. Two of my dreams had come true before I was nineteen years old.

My life up to that point had been so different, and was like a book with many chapters of learning experiences. Each teacher, each friend, and each family member taught me something different that I still cherish in my heart. Without learning from each of my experiences, I would not be the person I am today. I thank everyone who, in one way or another, molded me into the person that I have become. I call upon everyone to learn from his or her past mistakes, misfortunes, and even positive experiences. An individual would not grow wiser if it weren't for his or her unique life experiences.

Although the paycheck I received in the military was at times disappointing, given all my hard work, I never saw my time as a waste. I ran five miles a day with my battalion, routinely did pushups and situps, learned traditional military customs, and gained the strength of Superman (while only weighing 120 pounds). I dreamed of a better life, and saw education as a ticket to a more fulfilling life. I was one proud young man wearing a camouflage uniform and representing the Department of the Army. Private and then Specialist Vazquez were the names that I grew accustomed to hearing until my discharge.

During my duty years, I was in an accident in a military tank. It was around 2:00 a.m in the Mojave Desert during a night mission training. I heard the captain say that we had only minutes to move from our location because we were in enemy fire zone. Everyone rushed to take the nets down that covered the tanks and pack all items into the tank. Because it was so dark outside I could not see clearly. I was on top of the tank and fell into the driver's cockpit. I was the driver, so it was my duty to move the tank in a timely manner; regarless if I got hurt or not. The mission had to continue. No one heard the fall when I banged my knees into the driving gears. I looked at my knees and saw no blood or rips in my uniform. I was in so much pain that I could barely think, I just followed the instructions of my sergeant from my earphones. After that incident, I developed a condition known as patella femoral syndrome, which eventually hindered my duty requirements. Over time, I felt that my legs could not support my upper body, and the pain continued during the late night hours. It was painful to run and lift things. Even while sitting down I would feel pain. I developed multiple attacks of migraine headaches as well. Many times, I found myself crying in private due to the duty of not showing pain in public.

My best friend while I was stationed at Fort Hood was from Mexico. Julio would travel four hours from the military base to the border town of Del Rio, Texas. His family lived on both sides of the U.S.-Mexico border. He had just returned from his two-year overseas assignment at Camp Casey in Tongduchon, South Korea, so we understood each other, being so far away from our families. Corporal Cruz was only a year older than me and took me as a brother. His family treated me the same way. We worked together in the same unit and experienced the same stress out in the field. I've not forgotten eating his grandma's tamales when we paid her a visit in Mexico. To this day, I do not see him as a friend, but as my brother.

After many medical examinations during my tour of duty at Fort Hood, I was sent to a military panel of medical examiners and determined unfit for duty. I was then given orders to report back home in the spring of 1999. During several conversations with my mom, I asked her for advice in which career I should pursue, due to my medical condition. She stated that a career was something I would do for the rest of my life, and should be related to something I had a passion for. She was a nurse and cared for so many people. I wanted to help people as well, but in my case, I wanted to teach them about something I had a passion for. I knew I was good at art, and it was a longtime passion that came from my heart and soul. During that time, I applied to Southern Connecticut State University and decided to study to become a teacher. I was so excited when I received a letter from the university stating that I had been accepted into the art education program.

That summer, I attended my first class at Southern Connecticut State University in New Haven. It was a challenge, because I was wearing a cast, using crutches, and carrying a heavy backpack. Soon after my summer courses ended, I was scheduled for reconstructive foot surgery at the Veterans Affairs Medical Center in West Haven, Connecticut. During my convalescence, I learned to live confined to a wheelchair for several weeks, I developed the ability to demonstrate patience, and I grew to see life from a totally different perspective. My life had changed so much that I mentally and spiritually saw the glass as half full rather than half empty. In all of this, there was a lesson and experience that would change my life forever. Until that time, my experiences had shaped my personality, desires, and convictions into a reality from which I could not be deterred and in which I would not fail. I saw the color of my paint as being green, Army green. I would never forget the uniform I washed, ironed, and wore for five long years, and that would change my life forever. My dreams became a reality. I became a soldier, postal worker and was now on a journey in becoming an Art teacher. That is the color of my paint.

ENDNOTES

[1]   **Acerola** = small cherry-like fruit with a mild, sweet acid taste.

[2]   **Marquesina** = shelter area attached to a house.

[3]   **Recao** = sautéed, flavored herb used in Caribbean cooking.

[4]   **Sofrito** = a combination of ingredients used as a seasoning to give a distinctive flavor to many dishes.

[5]   **Coqui** = a native small frog located in Puerto Rico that makes the sound "coqui".

[6]   **Reinita** = native Puerto Rican bird.

[7]   **Viejo San Juan** = Old San Juan, historic colonial section of San Juan, Puerto Rico.

[8]   **Feliz Navidad** = Merry Christmas

[9]   **Guacamayo** = parrot; blue and yellow macaw species.

[10]   **Bendición** = blessings, usually said to elders out of respect.

[11]   **Abuela** = grandmother.

[12]   **Lechonera** = an eating establishment where pork meat is roasted on a spit over open fire.

[13]   **Morcillas** = Spanish-style blood sausage eaten in Spain and Latin America.

[14]   **Gandules** = Pigeon peas.

15 **Coquito** = Eggnog-like native beverage of Puerto Rico.

16 **Ponche** = cream-based beverage traditionally served during the December holiday season.

17 **Gallito** = children's game using the bean of the algarroba tree.

18 **Trompo** = wooden spinning top.

19 **Algarroba** = carob tree or its pods.

20 **Novelas** = Latin American televised soap operas.

21 **Sábado Gigante** = Giant Saturday; Televised Spanish family show broadcasted from Miami, Florida.

22 **Estofon** = one dedicated to reading and learning.

23 **The Little Rascals** = American comedy short films about a group of neighborhood children and their adventures.

24 **Urbanización** = Housing development or residential area.

25 **Pava** = traditional hat used by sugarcane cutters.

26 **Abuelo** = grandfather.

27 **Maizena** = cornstarch pudding.

28 **Raza** = race, group of people.

29 **Callejón** = alleyway.

30 **Pileta** = outdoor basin or sink.

31 **Guayabera** = short-sleeved lightweight shirt, traditionally worn untucked.

32 **Fiestas Patronales** = patron saint festivities – festival in honor of the town's patron saint.

33 **The Smurfs** = popular animated television series broadcasted during the 1980's.

34 **Nuestra Señora del Carmen** = Our Lady of Mount Carmel.

35 **Titi** = aunt.

36 **Dios te bendiga mijo** = God bless you, son.

37 **Serenata** = serenade.

38 **La Ciudad de la Eterna Primavera** = The City of Eternal Spring.

39 **Los Bravos** = the Braves – Baseball team of Cidra, Puerto Rico.

40 **Jíbaro** = Puerto Rican mountain-dwelling peasants.

41 **Cidreño** = citizens of Cidra.

42 **Mi pueblo** = my town.

43 **A Toda Maquina** = To All Machines; WIPR 6 – government sponsored televised school competition game show.

44 **Trovador** = Troubadour; a singer, especially of folk songs.

45 **Galleria de Telemundo** = Telemundo Art Gallery. Located in WKAQ-TV, channel 2. San Juan, Puerto Rico.

ABOUT THE AUTHOR

Mario Luis Vazquez was born in Caguas, Puerto Rico in 1976. His parents, Maria Lopez and Luis Angel Vazquez Sr., are from the town of Cidra, Puerto Rico, where the author also grew up. Mario moved to the United States after he graduated high school. After serving in the United States Army, he received his Bachelor's and Master's degrees in Art Education from Southern Connecticut State University. He received his Specialist in Education degree at Barry University. After living in Puerto Rico, Connecticut, and Texas, he now has settled in Florida. He is an artist, educator, and author. He works as a high school and college art educator. He enjoys teaching, traveling, and reading. For more information, visit www.mariolvazquez.com.

LEARNING MOMENTS
By Chapters:

ADDITIONAL RESOURCES

For additional learning resources please visit the **Virtual Art Classroom** at www.mariolvazquez.com. There you will find learning activities for each chapter of this book.

PERSONAL REFLECTIONS

Write down an experience you had in the past that has impacted you in some way. Express the feelings you felt and what you learned from that experience. As you write from your heart, relive that moment and visualize that experience all over again.

CREATIVITY EXERCISE

When you finish writing, create a drawing of your own personal memory. Cherish this memory as your own treasure and share it with someone you feel would learn from your experience. At that moment, you become a teacher to someone who will learn from your own real-life experience. Add color to your drawing and give life to your experience all over again.

Notes

Notes

Notes

Notes

Notes

Notes

Notes

Notes